The Book of Totally Useless Information

The Book of
Totally Useless
Information

by Don Voorhees

A CITADEL PRESS BOOK
Published by Carol Publishing Group

A Citadel Press Book
Published by Carol Publishing Group

Citadel Press is a registered trademark of Carol
Communications, Inc.

Editorial Offices: 600 Madison Avenue, New York, N.Y. 10022
Sales & Distribution Offices: 120 Enterprise Avenue, Secaucus,
N.J. 07094
In Canada: Canadian Manda Group, P.O. Box 920, Station U,
   Toronto, Ontario M8Z 5P9

Queries regarding rights and permissions should be addressed to
Carol Publishing Group, 600 Madison Avenue, New York, N.Y. 10022

Carol Publishing Group books are available at special discounts
for bulk purchases, for sales promotion, fund raising, or
educational purposes. Special editions can be created to specifications.
For details, contact: Special Sales Department, Carol Publishing
Group, 120 Enterprise Avenue, Secaucus, N.J. 07094

Illustrations by Don Voorhees and Cinde Hildebrant.

Manufactured in the United States of America
10 9 8 7 6 5 4 3 2 1

Library of Congress Cataloging-in-Publication Data

Voorhees, Donal A.
    The book of totally useless information / by Donal A. Voorhees.
        p.   cm.
    "A Citadel Press book."
    ISBN 0-8065-1405-1
    1. Questions and answers.   I. Title.
    AG195.V64   1993
    031.02—dc20   92-38786
                                                          CIP

To LISA, my inspiration

Special thanks to Lois Wallace for her technical assistance.

The Book of Totally Useless Information

Why do Scottish Highlanders wear kilts?

The Scottish kilt, which may look like a plaid skirt for men, was created as a useful multipurpose garment. Originally the kilt was one large rectangular piece of cloth, some fifteen feet long by five feet wide, called a philabeg. It was folded lengthwise, wrapped around the waist, and then belted in place. The remainder of the cloth was thrown over one shoulder and pinned. This skirtlike apparel gave the men of the Highlands unrestricted movement of their limbs while traversing its rugged terrain. Its creation, however, was actually a result of the poverty of the people and a scarcity of wool. The old kilts were very versatile, since they could be pulled over the head and shoulders during inclement weather or used as a blanket when sleeping outdoors. While we might think of a kilt as a "skirt," women never wear them. The Scotsmen, however, are not shy about wearing their kilts.

Today, a kilt is like a knee-length pleated skirt, with a separate matching plaid or blanketlike mantle, which is worn over the left shoulder and fastened with a brooch. The kilt has seven yards of wool and the plaid has four. The kilt should never be worn below the middle of the knee.

Included in this festive regalia is a purselike pouch, known as a sporran (the kilt has no pockets). There are also rules governing the use of sporrans. No fashion-conscious Scotsman would be caught wearing his day bag, which is made of leather, during the evening, when only a fur bag will do.

Other parts of the costume include a doublet (jacket), a bonnet (cap), brogues (shoes), and knee-high stockings. To complete the ensemble, a decorative pin is worn so the kilt does not come open and reveal the wearer's undergarments or lack thereof. The more macho kilt wearer may place a knife in his sock, as Scottish soldiers once wore kilts in battle.

The most important part of the costume is, of course, the tartan or plaid (pronounced played) cloth pattern. The differing designs of stripes and colors, on wool cloth, came to represent the different family clans of the Scottish High-

lands. As all the valleys in Scotland where people settled were isolated from one another by the surrounding hills, the inhabitants of each area became known as a clan and each had its own "sett" or tartan. Tartans date back to the 1200s and were also worn by the Irish, and the Celts of Europe.

The British outlawed the wearing of tartans and kilts in Scotland, in 1745 after the Jacobite Rebellion. Many tartan patterns were lost before the ban was lifted in 1782. The Scottish military was, however, allowed to continue to wear their tartan, and they do so today. Today Scottish descendants around the world carry on the traditions of old, wearing Highland dress at parades, weddings, and ethnic celebrations.

Ask a Scot if wearing skirts, brooches, and handbags is dignified for a real man, and they will say of course. Do they wear underwear beneath their woolen kilts? Conventional wisdom says yes, but to each his own. At least they don't have to shave their legs!

Why did ESSO change its name to EXXON?

ESSO was one of the most widely recognized and respected corporate symbols in the world. The reasons behind the changing of the name to the now familiar EXXON is a long and twisted story.

In 1859, a retired railroad conductor, Edwin L. Drake, drilled the first commercially successful oil well in the United States near Titusville, Pennsylvania. John D. Rockefeller entered the picture four years later and through a series of partnerships he helped create several companies, including Standard Oil of Ohio in 1870. By 1882, Rockefeller and his associate formed the Standard Oil Trust, a large conglomerate that controlled over 90 percent of the country's oil refining and pipelines. The Standard Oil Company of New Jersey was created later that year as an operating company of the Trust.

Standard Oil was accused by the media and government officials of engaging in illegal business practices that prevented fair competition from other, smaller oil companies. In 1892, the Ohio Supreme Court ordered the Standard Oil Company of Ohio to be removed from the Trust. The various companies of the Trust were operated separately until 1899, when they were all brought together again under the Standard Oil Company of New Jersey. At this time it served as a holding company for thirty-seven smaller companies, and was one of the richest companies in the world.

The federal government, however, broke up Standard Oil of New Jersey in 1911 when the Supreme Court ordered the company to dissolve under the provisions of the Sherman Anti-Trust Act. This action carved up Standard Oil and created thirty-four independent competing companies, several of which retained the name Standard Oil, plus a regional designation—Standard Oil of New Jersey, Standard of New York, or Mobil; Standard of Indiana, or Amoco; Standard of California, or Chevron; Standard of Kentucky; and Standard of Ohio, or Sohio (later Atlantic Richfield).

The court decree did not address the ownership or use of the Standard Oil name. The parent company, Standard Oil Company (New Jersey), now had many rivals in other regions of the country.

Shortly after World War I, Standard Oil of New Jersey, still a huge conglomerate, sought to unify all its marketing activities in the United States and abroad under one easily identifiable trademark. The name ESSO was chosen because it was short and suggested the initials of Standard Oil.

The ESSO trademark was registered in 1923, and is still used as a marketing symbol today in about one hundred foreign countries. The famous ESSO oval logo was introduced in 1933 and was used throughout the company's U.S. markets from Maine to Louisiana, and around the world. However, when ESSO tried to extend its operations to the Midwest in the early thirties, they encountered legal resistance from the Standard Oil companies already operating in that area.

Standard Oil of Indiana contended that "ESSO" meant "Standard Oil" to the public and that in the Midwest "Standard Oil" was their exclusive property. Trademark infringement litigation followed and the courts ruled in favor of Standard of Indiana, issuing a permanent injunction against the use of ESSO in the Midwest in 1937. This decision barred ESSO from fifteen states. Further litigation in the sixties against Standard Oil of Kentucky resulted in ESSO being barred from another five states, including the growing Florida market.

By 1969, the ESSO trademark and the corporate name, Standard Oil of New Jersey, could not be marketed in twenty states, with the possibility of being banned from another eleven states. Clearly the world-famous company had to do something drastic. Changing the company name was the obvious, albeit complicated solution.

A committee was formed to come up with a new na
identify with at home and abroad. The new word neede(
have good visual qualities, be easily pronounced in all majo
world languages, have no negative connotations, and be
completely unique and thus free of any impending legal
challenges.

After exhaustive consumer and legal research studies the
name EXXON was decided upon. It was essentially a new
word but close enough to ESSO to make consumer recognition a little easier. Still, a worldwide study found some six
hundred other companies that had similar looking or sounding names, and each had to be negotiated with to ensure no
infringement problems would occur.

Security around the new name was airtight until it was
officially announced in 1972. The public readily accepted the
name EXXON and it is now used throughout the country
and around the world.

The ESSO name is still used to market petroleum products
outside the United States. Not, however, because of any
foreign legal limitations, as may have been rumored, but due
to the substantial customer goodwill built up in the ESSO
trademark over the years.

Why are there seven days in a week, twenty-four hours in a day, sixty minutes in an hour, and sixty seconds in a minute?

There is no mathematical or astronomical reason for the
number of days in a week as there is for the number of days
or months in a year, which are determined by the movements
of the sun and moon, respectively.

The Babylonians were the first civilization to have a seven-
day week. They created a seven-day week so they could
devote one day a week to worship the seven heavenly bodies
that they knew—Mercury, Venus, Mars, Jupiter, Saturn, the
moon, and the sun.

Later in history, other cultures had weeks varying in

ir to ten days, depending on the frequency of
Roman farmers worked the fields for seven
to market on the eighth. Therefore, the
eight-day week.

modern seven-day week resulted from the spread of
Christianity. In the Book of Genesis, God created the world
in six days; on the seventh day (the Sabbath) He rested. The
word "Sabbath" is from the Babylonian "Sabattu," a word
that came into use during the Jewish captivity under the
Babylonians. The Jewish Sabbath is on Saturday, as was the
Romans'. The Romans considered Saturday, ruled by Saturn,
to be an unlucky day and thus chose it to be a day of rest.

During the French Revolution in 1792, France established
a ten-day week with three-week months. Each day had ten
hours consisting of one hundred minutes and each minute
was comprised of one hundred seconds. This system was
extremely logical (as was the metric system, also established
during the French Revolution). Alas, the system was used
only thirteen years, until Napoleon took power and returned
France to the old Gregorian system, in order to please the
Pope.

Regardless of the source, today we all use the seven-day
week.

We can also thank the Babylonians for the purely artificial
divisions of seconds, minutes, and hours. Again, any number
could have been chosen, but the Babylonians considered
sixty a mystical number because no lower number could be
divided by more numbers. Had the system of time divisions
been created recently, it would doubtless be based on a
system of tens, as is the modern metric system.

We have the Egyptians to thank for the crazy number of
hours in a day. They divided the night up into twelve
segments, corresponding with the rising of twelve different
stars or constellations over their eastern horizon. They had
ten divisions for daytime, representing the ten different
positions of the sun, and two more divisions for dawn and
dusk. This eventually became the twenty-four hour day that
we still are using.

Why is North Carolina called the "Tarheel State"?

One product North Carolina was famous for throughout its history was tar. During the Civil War many heated battles were fought in North Carolina and the local regiments were dedicated rebel soldiers. During one particularly fierce battle, several other Confederate troops began to retreat, leaving the North Carolina regiments to fight on alone. The North Carolinians became incensed at the retreating "cowards." Supposedly the North Carolinians yelled that they would put tar on the heels of the retreating rebels so they would stick better during the next battle.

Other versions of the story, not popular in North Carolina, have it that a brigade of North Carolina soldiers retreated from their position during the battle and were chided by a Mississippi brigade to tar their heels before the next battle.

Regardless of the origin, North Carolina is now proudly known as the Tarheel State.

Was there ever a real Aunt Jemima?

No. Aunt Jemima Pancake Mix has been a trademark for over one hundred years. It was created by Chris L. Rutt, in Saint Louis, Missouri. He wanted a product name to reflect the "festive spirit" long associated with pancakes. In 1889, he got the idea for the "Aunt Jemima" name from a dance tune used in a vaudeville show.

In the early years, the product was promoted through portrayal of the Aunt Jemima character. Nancy Green, a Chicago resident, created the first Aunt Jemima personality by demonstrating pancake preparation at the Chicago World's Fair in 1893. Her portrayal of Aunt Jemima took place prior to the company's acquisition by the Quaker Oats Company on January 15, 1926.

Through the years, women have represented this famous trademark for special promotions, but there never was an

actual person named Aunt Jemima promoting the pancake mix. The design trademark is an artist's conception, which is periodically updated to reflect a modernized image.

Why do jets traveling at high altitudes leave those long cloudlike trails in the sky, while lower-flying jets do not?

High-flying jet aircraft are often hard to see, but the trails they leave behind can be easily spotted. These trails are more properly called "contrails," because they are formed from condensed water vapor. Jet engines release water vapor into the air from their exhaust. The hot water vapor from the jet engines mixes with the cold air of the atmosphere and condenses into a cloudlike foggy trail. The phenomenon is more likely to occur higher in the sky, where the air temperature is lower. If the relative humidity of the surrounding air is high, the contrail can last for several hours. If the relative humidity is low, it will quickly evaporate and disappear.

Another type of contrail, an "aerodynamic contrail," can

be produced by the reduced pressure created by air flowing over the wing of a plane. The reduced pressure causes the air to cool rapidly and condense. This type of trail disappears quickly in the turbulent wake of the airplane.

What is the significance of the Mitsubishi company logo and the Subaru company logo?

The Mitsubishi logo, three diamonds in the shape of a propeller, is not an accidental arrangement. The Mitsubishi corporation dates back before the days of World War II. The company was a big manufacturer of aircraft most notably, and unfortunately for the American navy, the AGM, known as the Zero. (Zeros were the planes that were used to launch the attack on Pearl Harbor. Ironically, they were constructed with steel purchased from the United States.)

The Zero was introduced in 1936. At the start of the war it was the best naval fighter in the world. The appearance of the German F6F Hellcat fighter aboard U.S. aircraft carriers, in 1943, heralded the end of Japanese air superiority. The Hellcats were faster and more maneuverable than the Zero. In the last two years of the war they shot down 5,156 enemy aircraft, nearly 75 percent of all the U.S. Navy kills.

American industry rose to the Japanese challenge in the early 1940s, and was one of the primary catalysts for the U.S. victory in World War II. Mitsubishi has since succeeded in producing more peace-oriented machines. The company's propeller logo, however, a leftover from Japan's imperialistic days, still proudly adorns Mitsubishi's autos and electronics products.

Another Japanese auto manufacturer with an intriguing corporate symbol is Subaru. Its insignia is a group of six stars, which represents the Pleiades star cluster in the constellation Taurus. This star cluster is called "Subaru" in Japan.

Ancient peoples often attached an evil reputation to the

Pleiades. Black Sabbath and All Hallows' Eve were set to occur when the Pleiades reached their highest point at midnight in autumn. Many ancient cultures record the cluster as having seven stars, instead of six. Apparently, the seventh star has dimmed in recent times, as we can only see six with the naked eye. According to mythology, the seven stars were supposed to represent the seven daughters of Atlas, who held the world on his shoulders.

Today the six visible stars represent the six Japanese companies that merged in 1953 to produce autos. Recently, the logo has changed. Subaru has brightened one of the stars and moved it away from the others in the group. This brighter star symbolizes Alcyone, the brightest of the six stars in the Pleiades. Considering the constellation in which the Pleiades reside, one would think that Subaru would have named one of their car models Taurus. Ford, however, beat them to it.

The Mazda Corporation has no company symbol, but it does have an interesting name. The word Mazda comes from the Persian god of light, Ahura Mazda. In 1910, General Electric adopted the god's name and registered it as a trademark for its lamps and light bulbs. The Persians' belief is that Ahura Mazda created the 486,000 good or lucky stars that people are born under, as opposed to the 486,000 evil stars. Today, Mazda is the registered name of Mazda Corporation, maker of autos.

If you touch a piece of wood and a piece of metal, why does the metal always feel colder if both are the same temperature?

We all have noticed this phenomenon. If you walk through a room in your home, touch a piece of wood furniture, then touch a metal pipe or doorknob at the same temperature. The doorknob will probably feel colder. This is due to a simple property of physics called heat conduction.

Wood is a poor conductor of heat. When you touch it, it seems to feel about the right temperature. Metal, on the other hand, is an excellent conductor of heat. The metal quickly draws heat away from your skin and gives you the impression that it is cooler than it actually is.

Heat conduction also explains why you can put your hand into a hot oven and not be burned by the air inside, but feel extreme pain if you touch a metal cake pan at the same temperature. Here again, air is a much poorer conductor of heat than metal.

This is why most good insulating materials have plenty of large air spaces within them.

Why does extremely hot or extremely cold water sometimes feel the same?

Did you ever fill the bathtub with very hot water, then put your foot in and feel intense pain? The water, at first, almost feels cold instead of hot. Upon a moment's reflection you realize it is hot and yank your foot out, pronto! What caused this confusion in sensations?

The skin contains both temperature and pain receptors. The pain receptors are only sensitive to extreme hot and extreme cold. The brain experiences both these sensations in the same way. Therefore, very hot and very cold temperatures cause the same kind of pain and the brain has trouble distinguishing between the two.

The Georgetown University basketball team is known as the Hoyas. What is a Hoya?

Those of you who follow college basketball have undoubtedly asked yourself this question before. According to the

Georgetown University guidebook, the name Hoya derives from an old Georgetown cheer, "Hoya saxa!"—a slightly ungrammatical translation of "What rocks!" Hoya means "what" in Greek and saxa is a latin word for "rocks." There are several theories as to the origin of this phrase. Some say it began in the 1800s with Georgetown's baseball team, the Stonewalls. Others maintain it goes back to the early 1900s and was a cheer used at football games.

Regardless of its roots, the phrase was shortened in the 1930s to Hoyas, to identify Georgetown athletes. So actually, their basketball team could be thought of as the Georgetown "Whats." So what kind of mascot could a team called the "Whats" have? A bulldog, of course.

According to legend, Father Vincent S. McDonough, prefect of discipline at the school in the early 1920s, had a scrappy Boston bulldog who went with him to football games. A newspaper man who covered the team's games began to associate the dog with the Georgetown teams. Jack, as the dog was affectionately called, has been the mascot, in spirit at least, ever since.

Why does scratching an itch make it feel better?

The old saying goes that if your palm itches you will come into some money. Finding money may be nice but it won't do a thing for your itch. A good scratch will. An itch can be caused by almost anything—insects, dust particles, allergies, emotions, infections, etc. All itches result for the same reason: local stimuli are irritating the fibrous nerve endings on the upper layer of the skin. The brain interprets these stimuli as itches. Scratching can either remove the stimuli or cause pain in the area of the itch, which neutralizes the itching sensation in the spinal cord.

While we are on the subject of itches, why is it that shirt manufacturers insist on sewing their itchy labels on the inside of the collar, where they are guaranteed to rub against the back of our necks and make us itch all day long?

Why is "posh" a word used to describe something elegant or fashionable?

During the Victorian era, the British Empire was at its apex, with colonies all around the globe. Thus the old saying, "The sun never sets on the British Empire."

India was a popular destination for the wealthy British traveler. The only practical and luxurious way to get to India was aboard a cruise ship. The journey from London to Bombay or Calcutta was a long one. Ships had to follow the west coast of Africa down around the Cape of Good Hope and up the east coast of Africa toward India. Much of the trip was through hot, humid, tropical climates.

These ships may have been well-appointed, but the invention of air-conditioning was far off, and the only cool air one might expect was from ocean breezes and fans. Cabins tended to be hot and stuffy, so opening the portholes was the only way to get ventilation. On the trip out, the portholes on the port side of the ship faced land, and on the trip home, the portholes on the starboard side faced the land. Portholes facing land were considered more desirable for ventilation, shade, shelter from bad weather, and viewing purposes. British civil servants traveling to India on the Peninsular and Orient Steam Navigation Company line supposedly started this trend in cabin reservations.

Thereafter, it became trendy for the wealthy to pay extra for the privilege of staying in portside cabins on the way out and starboard cabins on the trip home. The acronym P.O.S.H. (port out, starboard home) was stamped on their baggage and eventually evolved into the word "posh," which came to mean elegant or fashionable.

Two other words that were originally acronyms are

"scuba" and "snafu." SCUBA stands for self-contained underwater breathing apparatus. SNAFU was short for an old army saying "situation normal, all f--ed up."

Why do the elephant and donkey represent the Republican and Democratic parties?

Neither creature is particularly regal or distinguished. How did they come to be the symbols of our national parties? One person is primarily responsible. A man named Thomas Nast was the most influential political cartoonist in U.S. history. He was the nineteenth-century version of Gary Trudeau, and worked for *Harpers Weekly* magazine as a political cartoonist.

Another political cartoonist first used the donkey to represent the Democratic party in 1837, when a cartoon appeared depicting President Andrew Jackson riding the beast. However, Nast is credited with popularizing this political symbol. In 1870, he drew a donkey labeled "the

Copperhead Press," to mock the Democratic newspapers who sympathized with the South.

Nast first used the elephant to represent the Republican party in a satirical cartoon. In 1874 the New York *Herald* reported that President Ulysses S. Grant intended to run for an unprecedented third term in 1876, and accused him of "Caesarism," referring to the famous Roman emperors. Several weeks later, the paper erroneously reported that animals from the New York City Zoo had escaped and were roaming around Central Park. On November 7, just before midterm elections, a Nast cartoon ran in *Harper's Weekly* depicting a donkey disguised as a lion and marked "Caesarism." The lion was scaring all the other animals that were loose in the park, including a huge elephant labeled "the Republican Vote." Nast's depiction of the two parties using these animals was not complimentary but it stuck, and they now proudly represent their respective parties.

Had Nast been alive for the 1992 presidential campaign, he might have chosen the dim-witted quail to represent the Republican party, and probably would still use the stubborn donkey for the Democratic party symbol.

Incidentally, Nast is also famous for drawing the first modern-looking Santa Claus. Before Nast, Santa didn't even have a beard.

Why is a left-handed pitcher known as a "southpaw?"

If left-handed pitchers are called southpaws, you would think right-handed pitchers might be called "northpaws." Obviously, this is not the case, but according to the story of the coining of the word southpaw, you would technically be right (correct, that is!).

In the latter part of the 1880s, Finley Peter Dunne, a sports writer with a sense of humor, was covering baseball games in Chicago. At one particular game, where home plate faced to the west, Dunne noticed that a left-handed pitcher released the ball with his hand (paw) that was to his south side. (It must have been a boring game!) Just like a lot of these dopey expressions, this one stuck and we now refer to all left-handers as southpaws. Apparently, Mr. Dunne did not see fit to call right-handers "northpaws."

Why is the sky blue?

We all take the beautiful blue color of our skies for granted. However, if Earth's atmosphere contained different gases this would not be the case. Air is made up of a mixture of gases in the following proportions: 78 percent nitrogen, 21 percent oxygen and 1 percent carbon dioxide and trace amounts of other gases.

The chemical composition of the gases in the air accounts for the color of the sky. The light coming to Earth from the sun contains all wavelengths and therefore all colors. Each color has its own wavelength—some are short, some are long. This is evidenced by rainbows, in which raindrops act as prisms, bending each wavelength of light at slightly different angles and causing the beautifully colored bands of light.

The longer wavelengths, yellow and red, reach our eyes in a nearly direct line from the sun. The shorter wavelengths, blue and violet, are more scattered by air molecules. This acts to diffuse the blue light, and it reaches our eyes from all parts of the sky, making the sky appear blue.

Hazy days occur when all wavelengths of light are scattered and bombard our eyes, thus making the sky appear whitish. Large amounts of water vapor in the atmosphere also scatter light, making very humid days tend to appear hazy.

If you look at the sun at midday (please don't try this!), it will look white. This is because all wavelengths of visible light will strike your eyes at noon. However, at sunset or sunrise the sun is at a much lower angle and its light has a lot more atmosphere to travel through to reach your eyes. At four degrees above the horizon, its light has twelve times more atmosphere to go through than at noon.

Large particles of dust filter out the blue light and the sun appears yellow-red. The cleaner the air, the more yellow the sun will be. After a good cleansing rainstorm, sunsets tend to be more yellow. The dirtier the air, the redder the sunset. Salt particles and water vapor account for the beautiful red sunsets often seen at the beach. Air pollution and volcanic eruptions add particles to the air and also create red sunsets. At times, the air is so polluted in some areas of the world that all wavelengths of visible light are scattered, and even red light can't penetrate. Since no visible light reaches the eyes, the sun literally disappears before it sets!

Smoke or ash particles of relatively uniform size can selectively filter sunlight, allowing certain colors through. For instance, it is not unheard of for the sun to appear green at midday, or even blue! A similar phenomenon is possible with moonlight and can result in the fabled and extremely rare blue moon.

Perhaps if we humans keep polluting the air and altering its chemical makeup, we may one day enjoy green or even brown skies on a daily basis.

What makes a quartz watch special?

Quartz is the most abundant mineral in the world, making up about 10 percent of the Earth's crust. It is composed of oxygen and silicon, the crust's most common elements. The form of quartz we are all most familiar with is sand. Quartz is extremely hard and is used in abrasives like sandpaper, in concrete, glass-making, porcelain, and sandstone building blocks.

Quartz also has one quality that makes it valuable to modern technology: it has an amazing property known as piezoelectricity. Like some other crystals, quartz crystals will generate an electric current when distorted by pressure.

The opposite is also true. Quartz changes shape when an electric current is applied to it. Alternating current will cause the crystal to vibrate microscopically at millions of vibrations per second. This piezoelectric effect enables quartz crystals to be used in modern watches to yield an extremely accurate and consistent timepiece. Quartz watches vary by only about 0.1 seconds, plus or minus, a year.

Quartz watches still require batteries to supply a charge to vibrate the crystals. A microchip reduces the rate of vibration to one pulse/second. This signal controls a tiny motor that operates the movement of hands or the display of digital numerals. Electrical currents produced by compressed quartz crystals are also used to ignite gas stoves, automobile engines, and explosive devices.

Why is it unsafe to go swimming immediately after eating?

This is another of those old wive's tales that your mother forced you to follow. All your friends would be frolicking in the water, coaxing you to come in while you stood there, looking stupid, explaining that you just ate and had to wait an hour to swim or you would get cramps and drown. Your friends would just laugh. Well, it turns out your friends may have had good reason to laugh. There is probably more chance of drowning on an empty stomach than a partially full one.

The old reasoning went that food being digested in your stomach took blood away from other parts of the body, including your muscles. This lack of blood could cause muscle cramps and drowning. In fact, a little food in your stomach is good. Food supplies glucose to your muscles, which increases your energy. Long-distance swimmers have known this for years and always eat a light meal before swimming.

The real danger of cramping up comes from cold water and fatigue. Eating can decrease fatigue and also stoke the body's furnace to help keep you warm. Just don't gorge yourself and then take the plunge, as too much food can make you drowsy and slow your reflexes.

What is the difference between bourbon and Scotch?

Both are forms of whiskey. Bourbon is of American manufacture, distilled from corn. Scotch, as you probably know, is made in Scotland from barley. Scotch's distinctive taste comes from the smoking of the barley malt over peat fires before distillation. Bourbons, by law, must be at least 51 percent corn mash. The kinds of grain making up the other 49 percent can be varied, giving different bourbons their own unique flavors.

There are straight and bonded bourbons, but most Scotches are blended "straight"—without the use of other alcohols.

Both Scotch and bourbon are not acceptable unless they are aged for at least four years.

Why are strikeouts in baseball referred to as K's?

In the 1860s, when a player struck out, instead of saying "he struck out" they said "he struck." Baseball box scores were kept back then, as they are today. Letters were used to indicate what a player did. E stood for error, S for sacrifice, etc. Since S was already used for sacrifice, Henry Chadwick, the inventor of box scores in 1880, designated the last letter of struck, K, to represent striking out.

Why does moss grow on the north side of trees?

As every good Boy Scout or Girl Scout should know, you can tell which direction you are traveling in the woods by observing tree trunks. Moss has a tendency to grow on the north side of trees.

The sun is responsible for this occurrence. In the middle latitudes of the Northern Hemisphere the sun rises in the southeast and sets in the southwest during the winter. In summer, it rises in the northeast and sets in the northwest. Objects that face south, therefore, receive more sunlight throughout the year than those facing north, a fact which is readily evident on mountain slopes as well as on trees. North-facing mountain slopes tend to be moister and cooler than the sunnier south-facing slopes. For this reason, in many areas like the Far West, the vegetation is much lusher and greener on northern slopes.

Moss likes the cool, moist conditions that exist on the northern side of trees and often will grow more abundantly there. However, this is not a totally reliable way to navigate through the woods. Better to pack a compass.

Boy and Girl Scouts aren't the only ones to use this effect of the sunlight to their advantage. Wine growers in New York State, knowing that the growing season is longer on southern slopes, plant their grapes there to get a better product. Conversely, ski slopes are built on the north face of mountains whenever possible, because the snow lasts longer there.

Why do cars in some countries drive on the left side of the road, and in others on the right?

The custom of driving on the left or right side of the road varies from country to country, and its origins predate the invention of the automobile. During the 1700s, in England, horse-drawn coaches were the main mode of transportation for urban dwellers. British coachmen used to sit on a seat on the right side of the carriage. If the coach traveled down the right side of the road, the coachman's whip would have hit pedestrians strolling along the adjacent sidewalk. By keeping to the left, the coachman had room to use his whip and the pedestrians were safe. The coach drivers could just as easily have sat on the left side and driven on the right, but that is not the way it turned out.

Cars in France, England's neighbor, drive on the right side of the road for reasons also related to the horse and buggy. Eighteenth-century French coachmen rode on the left side of the pair of pulling horses, and drove on the left side of the road. This caused the horses to pull to the left and up onto the sidewalk. They were subsequently ordered to stay to the right to protect pedestrians.

It makes practically no difference today which side of the road is driven on, as long as everyone uses the same side!

Why has Switzerland traditionally been a neutral country?

Today, Switzerland is a peace-loving, perennially neutral country. The Swiss have not always been such a docile people. During the 1700s, Switzerland lost one-third of its population due to wars and the death of many of its mercenary soldiers. The decision to become a nation of pacifists may have been prompted more by self-survival than by altruism.

In fact, the Swiss government is so concerned with the survival of its people that they still have a program to build enough bunkers to protect the entire population of 6.8 million people in the event of a nuclear attack, even though the cold war has finally ended.

Why is thirteen of something known as a baker's dozen?

Bread has been the staff of life since ancient times. By the middle of the twelfth century A.D., the baking industry in England had become very organized, and London bakers had formed an official brotherhood. Later, they reorganized into the Company of Brown Bakers and the Company of White Bakers and were subject to very strict regulations. A law passed in 1266 stipulated that exactly eighty loaves of bread were to be baked from a standard sack of flour. It was illegal to sell loaves of bread that varied from a set weight. Bakers who were found selling underweight loaves to retailers could get in big trouble. There are stories of bakers in the Middle East who were nailed by their ears to their shop's doorway for selling underweight bread! Adding an extra loaf of bread for every twelve they sold, to make up for any underweight loaves, was a small price for the bakers to pay.

What does "hermetically sealed" mean?

We hear this term used to describe something that has an airtight seal, such as the answer envelopes that Ed Mac-Mahon would give to the Great Karnak (Johnny Carson) to hold up to his head to divine the questions inside.

The expression "hermetically sealed" comes from about the third century A.D. Hermes Trismegistus, meaning Hermes thrice greatest (three times greater than the original Greek god Hermes), was said to have been the Egyptian god of wisdom, Thoth. Hermes supposedly dictated twelve *Hermetic Books* to mystic philosophers, containing secrets for alchemists. One of the secrets contained in the books was how to magically seal a vessel so that no air could get in.

Today, there is nothing magical or special about containers that are hermetically sealed. It is simply a fancy way of saying airtight, which honors the ancient god Hermes.

From where does porterhouse steak derive its name?

Porterhouse steak is a cut of beef loin adjacent to the sirloin, which is more succulent but has a lot of waste. In England, no distinction is made between porterhouse and sirloin. An American named Martin Morrison gave porterhouse steak its name. In 1814 he ran a New York City tavern called Martin Morrison's Porterhouse, which specialized in this cut of beef.

A porterhouse was a tavern that served dark beer and ale, called porter supposedly because it was a favorite drink of porters and laborers. Ironically, these blue-collar workers could seldom afford to eat a porterhouse steak.

Who was "Uncle Sam"?

When we picture Uncle Sam today, we picture a man with a long white beard, red-and-white striped pants, and a blue jacket. There was an "Uncle Sam," but he looked nothing like this, although he did wear a top hat and he did come to be a symbol of the U.S. government.

Sam Wilson supplied the U.S. troops stationed around

Troy, New York, with meat during the War of 1812. The meat shipped to the soldiers was stamped "U.S." for the United States. One day, when a federal inspector was checking the meat at Wilson's store, he was told by a witty employee that the "U.S." stood for Uncle Sam, Wilson's nickname. It was not long before all federal supplies were said to belong to "Uncle Sam."

While this story was thought to be contrived, an 1830 newspaper article quotes eyewitnesses who swear it's true. In the early 1960s Congress made it official, proclaiming Sam Wilson as the original Uncle Sam.

Why aren't any two snowflakes alike?

How could it be that no two snowflakes are identical? It seems pretty improbable when you consider that a rough estimate of the numbers of snowflakes that have fallen on the Earth throughout its history is about 1,000,000,000,000,000, 000,000,000,000,000,000,000. That's a lot of snowmen!

There are about eight to one hundred different recognized classes of snowflakes. Most are variations on the basic hexagonal shape that water molecules assume when frozen. When water molecules freeze, they form an ordered arrangement based on the sixty-degree angles assumed by the oxygen atoms relative to the hydrogen atoms. If you enlarged a frozen water molecule about a billion times it would resemble the head of Mickey Mouse, the "head" being the oxygen atom, the "ears" being the two hydrogen atoms.

Shapes within this basic hexagonal arrangement can vary greatly. Snowflakes can be thick or thin starlike plates, with different branching patterns (dendrites); columnar, needle-like, or irregular.

A snowflake needs a nucleus around which to form. This is usually a speck of dust, sea salt, or some other particle in a snow cloud. Water vapor molecules accumulate and freeze on the airborne particles. As they start to grow into ice crystals, they are blown around and begin to fall toward Earth, all the while gathering more water droplets and growing into larger ice crystals. What makes snowflakes unique from one another is the slightly different conditions of temperature and moisture under which each flake is born and develops. No two specks of dust are truly identical and the microclimate each flake passes through in the cloud is slightly different from that for others.

For example, the temperature and moisture content of snow clouds vary from one point in space to another, and no snowflake is born in exactly the same space or travels exactly the same path in its development. These might seem like minor differences, but they are enough to make all snowflakes different.

Snowflakes that are created at 32° to 27° F are hexagonal plates, at 27° to 23° needle shapes form, at 23° to 18° hollow prismatic columns form, at 18° to 10° hexagonal plates again form, at 10° to 3° fernlike stars (dendrites) form, at −3° to −13° plates form, and at −13° to −53° hollow prismatic columns form. Snowflakes only form at these relatively mild temperatures. The polar regions are too cold and rarely receive snowflakes. Usually all they get is snow dust.

From time to time, similar snowflakes are found. They look to the eye to be the same, but upon closer examination, there will be slight differences. After all, snowflakes have about a billion billion molecules. If two were ever identical, now that would be truly amazing!

Are foods labeled "natural" really all natural?

There are no federal guidelines governing the use of the word natural. Foods labeled as "natural" can contain artificial preservatives, coloring, flavoring, and other additives. One trick food processors use is to advertise a "natural American cheese" product. While the cheese part may be natural, the rest of the product can contain artificial anything.

Other food-labeling words are explained below.

- "Sugar free" products contain no sugar, but may contain other sweeteners that have calories, such as corn syrup, fructose, dextrose, or honey.
- "Reduced calories" means the product must contain one-third less calories than a comparable food product.
- "Low calorie" means the product cannot have more than forty calories per serving.
- "No preservatives" means there are no artificial preservatives, but artificial colors and flavors are allowed.
- "Fortified" and "enriched" indicate that some of the nutrients processed out of the food have been put back in, but not necessarily all of them. This is usually the case with "fortified and enriched" breads and flours.

Most foods are required to list ingredients on the label. They are listed in order of their weight in the final product. If sugar is listed first, it is the main ingredient. Even "fresh" vegetables and fruits will contain pesticides, color enhancers, waxes, etc. Only hard-to-find "organically" grown produce is free of these nasties. Still, if you worry about what goes into your food, grow your own.

Which planet is the farthest from the sun?

If you say Pluto, you are only half right. Actually, at the time of this book's publication, Neptune is the farthest planet from the sun! Although Pluto, on average, is about 3.6 billion miles from the sun, its orbit is not circular but elliptical, with the effect that its distance from the sun varies. At its minimum distance, Pluto is only 2.7 billion miles from the sun, less than that of Neptune, which lies at an average distance of 2.8 billion miles. Neptune will remain the farthest planet until 1999.

What really happened at the Alamo?

The Alamo was built by Franciscans between 1716 and 1718. The building originally served as the chapel of the Mission San Antonio de Valero. By 1801 the Franciscans had abandoned the mission, and Spanish troops sporadically occupied the deteriorated building. It was at this time that the old chapel became known as "the Alamo," from the grove of cottonwood (*alamo* in Spanish) in which it stood.

Texas was a Mexican colony. However, by 1835, over thirty thousand Americans had settled there and they far outnumbered the resident Mexican population. The Americans living in Texas at the time were an independent bunch and tended to shun the Mexican government. To bring the Texans into the Mexican fold, the government imposed martial law and tried to disarm the Americans. Hostilities inevitably followed. The war for Texan independence had begun.

In December 1835, a small detachment of Texan volunteers drove a Mexican force from San Antonio and occupied the Alamo. Sam Houston, commander of the Texan forces, recommended abandoning the Alamo, as it was impossible to defend with such a small force. The heroic volunteers, however, refused to leave their exposed position. On February 23, 1836, Mexican general Antonio Lopez de Santa Anna led over six thousand Mexican soldiers in a siege against the Alamo. The 182 Americans, including Davy Crockett and Sam Bowie, who were holed up in the Alamo, refused to surrender. The garrison defiantly held their position until March 6, when Santa Anna stormed the building from all sides and overwhelmed the defenders in hand-to-hand combat inside the Alamo.

As every student knows, all the Texans defending the old church from the Mexicans died in the heat of battle, fighting to the very last man. The Mexicans, meanwhile, lost about fifteen hundred men.

This famous battle is a source of American pride and the

Texan rallying cry, "Remember the Alamo!" However, according to historians, the evidence suggests that Crockett and several others were actually captured by Santa Anna and tortured before being executed. Supposedly, Mexican general Manuel Fernandez Castrillon wanted to spare the Texans but Santa Anna refused. The reason the defenders may have tried to hold out for so long was that they were expecting to be rescued by reinforcements any day. The fact that they were indeed captured while waiting for reinforcements in no way takes anything away from those brave men fighting to defend their country. Any logical person facing those odds would have surrendered immediately. The Texans lost this battle but later went on to win the war in 1836 and became the Republic of Texas. In 1845, Texas was annexed by the United States and became the twenty-eighth state.

Interestingly, most of the "Texans" who died fighting for independence had never been in Texas before the first few weeks of 1836. Most of the men who lived in Texas prior to the revolution chose not to join the army. So much for Texan pride!

Why couldn't Chevrolet sell the Nova in South America?

American auto companies do not take the names of their new cars lightly. Automakers usually do extensive market research and enlist the help of the multimillion-dollar advertising industry when choosing the nameplate to bolt on their autos. It is mind-boggling to think that one of the largest corporations in the world, General Motors, could make a blunder as big as the one they made in naming the Chevy Nova two decades ago. Some "genius" came up with the name Nova for one of their new cars, which, appropriately enough, means "new" in Latin.

After Chevy launched the sales campaign, company executives puzzled over the terrible sales for this model in Mexico and South America, until it was pointed out to them that Nova in Spanish means "no go" or "it doesn't go"! This major gaffe could have been averted had any GM executive paid attention during high school Spanish I. After they changed the name to "Caribe," sales increased.

This episode is a classic example of how American industry used to live with its collective head in the sand when it came to selling to foreign markets. In today's world, cultural isolation is a luxury the United States can no longer afford. This is a concept that West Germany and Japan grasped long ago. These two countries export a far greater percent of their gross national product than does the United States. The Germans and Japanese took the "trouble" to learn about the culture of the foreign countries that they marketed products for. Meanwhile, American business got fat and lazy. Sometimes you have to learn the hard way.

Here are some other classic examples of American business ignorance:

- A "Body by Fisher" ad for a General Motors product in Europe read "Corpse by Fisher" in Flemish.
- A "Come Alive With Pepsi" ad came out "Come Alive Out of the Grave" in German.

Even that most "competent" of presidents, Jimmy Carter, made a linguistic faux pas. When visiting Poland, Carter tried to say "I wish to learn your opinions and understand your desires for the future." What he actually said in Polish was "I desire Poles carnally."

How did Chicago come to be called the "Windy City?"

While Chicago is one of the windier cities in the United States, with an average wind speed of 10.3 miles per hour, its moniker, "Windy City," has nothing to do with the wind. In 1893, Chicago hosted the World's Columbian Exposition, honoring the 400th anniversary of Christopher Columbus's arrival in the New World. The underlying reason for hosting the fair was to show off the city's accomplishments. So boastful and overblown were the local politicians' claims about the exposition and the city, that a New York City newspaper editor, Charles A. Dana, nicknamed Chicago the "Windy City." The fact that Chicago was, indeed, a windy city, helped the name stick.

It was the city's strong winds that on October 8, 1871, fanned the flames of the Great Chicago Fire, which spread from a barn owned by Mrs. Patrick O'Leary, eventually destroying much of the city. Whether her cow actually was the cause is not certain. On the brighter side, the winds blowing in off Lake Michigan bring fresh air to the crowded city streets. They may need it. The name Chicago derives from an Algonquin Indian word meaning "garlic field," "place of the bad smell," or "skunktown"!

What is the origin of the legend that storks bring babies?

This legend started in Germany and Sweden long ago. Every spring, white storks return to Europe from their wintering grounds in Africa. Upon their return, the storks seek out suitable nesting sites to raise their young. Frequently, they build their large nests on high chimneys or rooftops. Since the storks return every spring, the citizens believed that they brought good luck and that a stork's nest on top of one's house was a sign of good fortune or fertility for the occupants. To avoid telling young children the facts of life, adults would explain that storks deliver babies and that mother needed bed rest after the delivery because she was bitten by the bird.

Storks can be quite heartless parents. If food supplies are low, the youngest born hatchlings will usually starve to

death and be cast from the nest, or even be eaten by an indifferent parent!

What is the origin of the saying "bury the hatchet"?

Native Americans were still living in the Stone Age before they were conquered by the white man. One popular Native American weapon was a sharpened, chipped stone tied to a wooden handle. Europeans called this war club a tomahawk, after an Algonquian word for it. While this crude but effective weapon was ridiculed by the white man, it was an object of great ceremony to the tribes of the Northeast. When a dispute was settled, many tribes would bury a tomahawk as a symbolic gesture of peace. If hostilities were renewed, the tomahawk would be dug up, representing a declaration of war.

All Native American tribes did not practice the ritual of burying a tomahawk, but those that did took it seriously. It was easily a more binding peace ceremony than the shameful "peace" treaties that the white man continually made with them and subsequently broke.

Today, the expression "bury the hatchet" can be used in reference to the resolution of any argument. It is common to ask your mate, after a disagreement, if he or she wants to bury the hatchet. If the reply is that he or she would like to bury it in the back of your head, you might want to try again later.

Why do we call physically attached twins "Siamese twins"?

The first attached twins who gained notoriety were actually from Siam (Thailand). Chang and Eng Bunker were born attached at the chest in 1811. They were discovered sixteen years later and subsequently brought to the United States by master promoter P. T. Barnum. He billed them as the world-renowned "Chinese Double-Boys." The two argued often with Barnum and between themselves, only doing exhibits when they needed money.

They married English sisters, Adelaide and Sarah Yates, in 1864. Between them they had twenty-two children: Chang ten and Eng twelve. It is not known what their sleeping arrangements were, but the situation must have been interesting, if not a bit tricky.

The two families settled down in New Hampshire, where the twins died in 1874, within hours of each other. Since they had a shared circulatory system, the death of one spelled doom for the other.

Chang and Eng were so well known that all attached twins, or even inseparable friends, became known as Siamese twins.

Are certain people really double-jointed?

Growing up, we all knew the kids who could gross us out by bending their thumb back to their wrist or bending their legs behind their heads. We refer to these people as double-jointed.

In reality no one is double-jointed. Contortionists actually are able to stretch the ligaments that surround certain joints, which would normally restrict their movements. By doing stretching exercises, these people can further exaggerate their unique ability. For some reason, females are more often double-jointed than males.

Is the Mercedes-Benz auto company named after the two men who founded it?

Carl Benz and Gottlieb Daimler were two early rival automobile pioneers working in Germany during the 1890s. Daimler patented the gasoline internal combustion engine in 1883. He was more concerned with engine design than auto design. Benz invented the first gasoline-powered motor vehicle and concentrated most of his efforts on car designs. In 1889, Daimler developed the first four-wheeled car. They had all been three-wheeled prior to this.

Auto racing became a very popular sport among the rich at the end of the nineteenth century, and this prompted the continued development of the industry. A valued Daimler customer, Emil Jellinek, consul general in Nice for the Austro-Hungarian Empire, convinced Daimler to design a new racing car for him in 1900. Daimler named the new car "Mercedes" in honor of Jellinek's daughter, Mercedes. The car was a big success and the name Mercedes stayed with the company ever since.

In 1926, when the rival Daimler and Benz companies

joined forces, the new company was called Mercedes-Benz. Although Carl Benz and Gottlieb Daimler worked only sixty miles from each other, they never met.

Why are you supposed to open the windows of your house during a tornado?

Each year, almost eight hundred tornadoes touch down in the United States and claim around 190 lives. One midwestern tornado claimed 689 lives in three hours' time, on March 18, 1925.

Folks in the Midwest get more than their share of tornadoes. Most occur in a wide swath of land known as "Tornado Alley," which runs from the Texas panhandle, northeast through Oklahoma, Kansas, Missouri, Nebraska, and parts of Illinois and Iowa.

People in the Midwest have been taught since childhood to open the windows, and run into the basement during tornadoes. The rationale was that during a tornado a sudden drop in air pressure would cause the house to explode if it was shut up tight. Recently, however, meterologists have realized that opening the windows does not do that much to equalize the pressure, as most houses are fairly well ventilated anyway.

Houses do not really explode during a tornado as was thought. They are blown apart by its one-hundred-plus-mile-per-hour winds. Opening the windows actually can do more damage to your home than good. If a tornado just misses your house, the open windows can contribute to your home's destruction. The strong winds of a tornado blowing on a house can cause a pocket of low pressure on the opposite side, which tugs outward on the leeward wall. If the windows on the windward wall are open, it allows the winds to blow through the house and push out on the leeward wall, helping to topple the house.

While the advice to open the windows may have been wrong, the part about going to the basement is still valid. It is the safest place to seek shelter from a tornado. Tornado season lasts from spring to early summer.

Tornadoes form when warm, moist air from the Gulf of Mexico becomes trapped beneath cooler heavier air from the Rockies. The warm air tries to rise and the cool air tries to descend, and severe thunderstorms ensue. Occasionally the warm air below breaks through the cool air cap above and violently rushes upward, causing a tornado. Wind speeds can reach from two hundred to five hundred miles-per-hour and can drive a piece of straw into a tree trunk, like a nail!

The average tornado leaves a path of destruction about one thousand feet wide and several miles long. Thankfully, they are short-lived, dying out in about twenty or thirty minutes. Tornado paths vary in length from a few feet to nearly three hundred miles, but average about five miles. The diameter of tornadoes averages about six hundred and fifty feet but can be anywhere from a few feet to over one mile. Their average forward speed is about thirty miles per hour. Seventy-five percent of tornadoes occur from March to July. The month of May has the most, about four a day, but the most violent tornadoes usually strike in April. Tornadoes are most common between 4:00 and 6:00 P.M., when the surface air is most unstable. They are least likely to develop before dawn, when the air is more stable.

While the notion that an entire house could be picked up and carried to some far-off land, as in *The Wizard of Oz*, is pure fantasy, tornadoes have accomplished some impressive and unusual feats. A railroad car carrying over one hundred people was once picked up and deposited some eighty feet away. Another tornado destroyed a schoolhouse and transported its eighty-five students over three hundred feet away—no one was killed. And while it may never have rained cats and dogs, it has rained toads and frogs, after they had been sucked out of a pond by a tornado.

Why does the Dutch homeland have two names, Holland and the Netherlands?

Since the sixteenth century, the official name of the Dutch homeland has been the Netherlands. It is often incorrectly referred to by foreigners as Holland. This is because the people of the Netherlands call themselves Hollanders or Nederlanders. Again, the English-speaking world insists on calling them Dutch, much to their consternation.

Holland is actually only one small region of the Netherlands. This province, which comprises 16 percent of the national land area, was the center of the nation's wealth and home to many of the early Dutch explorers who traveled the world's oceans during the sixteenth century. Because these sailors called themselves Hollanders, foreigners inferred that they must have come from a country called Holland.

The Dutch people became so offended by the invasion of the English language over the last three centuries that, in 1934, their government officially banned the use of the word Dutch, mandating the use of the word Netherlands whenever possible.

The use of the word "Dutch," in the English language, to represent something inferior, is one example of what the Dutch resent. For instance, "Dutch treat" means a meal where everyone pays their own way, and "in Dutch" means in trouble. Early Americans also slighted the Dutch, mistakenly calling the German settlers of Pennsylvania "Dutch," instead of the German word "Deutsch," meaning German.

All this friction between the Dutch and the English goes back to 1624 when Dutch soldiers attacked the English at Amboina, East Indies. Not content to beat the English, the Dutch went on to massacre the survivors. England was furious but was in no position to retaliate. The Dutch attacked the English again in 1653 and sailed through the English Channel, arrogantly savoring their victory.

Another war broke out in 1665. These and other incidents

made the English hate everything Dutch. They ridiculed their enemy by calling anything spurious "Dutch."

Happily, William of Holland married Princess Mary of England in 1677, and the two countries patched things up. However, the ethnic slurs lived on.

Another interesting thing about the Netherlands is that it has two capital cities, The Hague and Amsterdam. In 1795, invading French troops captured Amsterdam and made it the capital. They renamed the country the Batavian Republic. In 1806, Napoleon I changed it to the Kingdom of Holland. The Dutch drove the French out in 1813 and restored their government in The Hague in 1814. However, the capital stayed in Amsterdam, where it remains today.

Is it really illegal to kill a praying mantis?

In most states you may kill a praying mantis as freely as you would any other insect, if you feel so inclined. The myth of the praying mantis being protected by law is a common one. Many of us were taught this at a very early age by well-intentioned people. Squash one mantis and the bug police would come knocking at your door with a fine ranging from fifty to five hundred dollars.

The early Greeks believed the praying mantis had supernatural powers and ancient seers "consulted" them. In fact, the word "mantis" comes from the Greek word for "prophet."

Our modern praying mantis myth probably came about because the mantis is such a beneficial insect to mankind. Mantises eat many harmful insects. If you are a gardener or a farmer you may want to go out of your way to protect this fiendish-looking bug. If not, a few less mantises in the world won't throw the ecosystem out of balance (anyway, the "destructive" insects have to make a living too!). Mantises, after all, are not the kindest of insects, eating almost anything that moves. Some of the larger tropical species will eat small birds, lizards, and frogs. They are voracious eaters who are never satisfied. The female mantis will even eat the male during mating! If you were only a half-inch tall, the mantis would not hesitate to devour you also!

What is "Cinco De Mayo"?

Most Americans had never heard of Cinco De Mayo (Fifth of May) until recently, when Dos Equis Beer began a sales promotion campaign encouraging all of us to drink their brew each May 5 in celebration of this Mexican holiday. Dos Equis, however, doesn't bother to tell us why we should celebrate Cinco De Mayo. Those of you who feel guilty about drinking for no apparent reason will be happy to know that Cinco De Mayo is, indeed, a legitimate Mexican holiday, not just a day created by a Mexican beer company to sell its product.

The Fifth of May is a great day in Mexican history. That day is the anniversary of the Battle of Guadaloupe near Puebla, where, in 1862, a Mexican army of about two thousand defeated a French force of six thousand.

Mexico had defaulted on bond payments and in 1861 French, Spanish, and British sent naval fleets to Vera Cruz to force payments to bondholders. A conference was held and the Mexicans agreed to pay up. The British and Spanish fleets, having accomplished their mission, sailed for home. The French, alas, had other intentions. They repudiated the agreement and set about to conquer Mexico. It was then, on May 5, 1862, that the French army was repulsed by a small Mexican force under the command of Ignacio Zaragoza. The victory was a minor one, as the French went on to conquer the country and place Emperor Maximillian on the throne. He was later deposed and shot.

The Mexicans may have won the battle and lost the war, but that one victory apparently was enough cause to establish a national holiday celebration.

Today, Cinco De Mayo is celebrated by Mexicans at home and abroad. The highlight of the day is a festive afternoon dinner, all-night dancing, and, of course, plenty of Mexico's finest beer and tequila.

Why is a score of zero in tennis called "love"?

This tennis term is not very lovely for the players. But, no matter; the word's origin has nothing at all to do with amore.

Love is really a distortion of the French word *oeuf*, which means egg, as in goose egg. Love is definitely a kinder way of referring to zero points than goose egg.

How does salt melt ice?

Each winter, countless tons of rock salt are spread on the roads and sidewalks of the world. Miraculously, salt has the ability to melt solid ice on a frigid day. No chemical reaction between the salt and ice takes place. It is more of a physical reaction.

Ice usually has a very thin layer of water on top of it. When salt is thrown on ice, some of it dissolves into this thin layer of water, forming a thin layer of salt water, which has a lower freezing point than fresh water.

When the salt goes from its solid state into solution, a little heat is released, which melts another thin layer of ice, allowing more salt to dissolve and create more saltwater. The process goes on and on, and slowly melts the ice.

Why does a circle have 360 degrees?

We can thank the Egyptians for this. While a circle could have been divided up into any convenient number of degrees, the Egyptians chose 360, one degree for each of the solar days in the Egyptian year (they added five days a year to correct their calendar).

In fact, our degree sign (°) is actually an ancient symbol of the sun. The degree was used to measure the distance through the Zodiac that the sun traveled each day, just as an astrological sign described the astronomical space the sun passed through in a month.

Did Betsy Ross really sew the first official American flag?

When the Continental army began forming, each militia had its own unique flag, but these were seldom flown. In those days, flags were usually flown by navies, not armies. In 1776, a common flag was adopted for use: the British Meteor, which had six horizontal white stripes added across a red field (the British flag, of course, had the Union Jack in the upper corner). Our version was known as the Grand Union, or Continental Flag.

After the signing of the Declaration of Independence, this flag, with its obvious British influence, fell out of favor. On June 14, 1777, the Marine Committee of the Second Continental Congress resolved that "the flag of the United States

be made of thirteen stripes, alternate red and white; that the union be thirteen stars, white on a blue field, representing a new constellation." The resolution did not define the arrangement or sizes of the stars and stripes and thus it was open to interpretation.

Various flag designs were created and flown in every conceivable arrangement. Several were variations on the Grand Union flag theme, while others actually had vertical stripes! It wasn't until forty-one years later that Congress specified that the stripes should be horizontal. It took until 1912 before the exact specifications of the flag were defined, in an executive order by President William Howard Taft.

The Betsy Ross legend is a cute story but highly unlikely. Supposedly, George Washington was ordered by Congress, in 1776, to design a flag. He gave a rough sketch to Betsy Ross, a Philadelphia seamstress, who modified the stars and created the flag. But Washington was very busy with the military at this time and it is doubtful he would have had the time to design a flag and contact Mrs. Ross. There is no Congressional record of Washington being ordered to design a flag. Furthermore, the Betsy Ross story was unheard of before 1870.

A more legitimate claim to designing that flag was made by a patriot named Francis Hopkinson. He was an artist who helped design U.S. currency and official seals. Hopkinson even billed Congress for his work on the flag, asking only for a "quarter cask of the public wine." Congress, however, never paid, citing that "he had not been the only one to work on the project." So apparently, Hopkinson was not the sole designer of the flag, but he obviously had some involvement.

In 1795, Congress passed the Second Flag Law, adding two stars and two stripes to the flag to recognize the admissions to the Union of Vermont and Kentucky. By 1818, Congress realized that with the increasing number of states to be admitted, there would soon be an unappealing number of stripes crowded together. So, they passed the Third Flag Law, whereby the number of stripes was returned to the original thirteen, but a star was to be added for each new state.

Today we have fifty stars, which fit very neatly on the blue field. If another state is added, bringing the number of stars to fifty-one, they will need a computer to figure out a new symmetrical arrangement.

Why is January 1 the first day of the year?

There is nothing special about January 1. It is simply the day we designate as the first day of the year. We could just as easily have picked any other day to start the year. In fact, March 1 began the Roman New Year until 153 B.C. In that year, new consuls took over the government on January 1 and decreed that date would begin the new year. However, it made more sense to begin the year in spring, when life was renewing itself, so the farmers and priests still observed the old new year.

In 46 B.C. Julius Caesar was at the height of his power and found that the Roman calendar had slowly drifted ahead of the solar calendar during the previous two hundred years. Religious planting festivals that were at one time observed in the spring were being celebrated in the summer.

Clearly, something had to be done. The religious calendar of the time was a lunar one (they considered the moon more important than the sun) with 355 days. Caesar declared January 1, the day new consuls took office, as the first day of the year. He also added ten days to the lunar calendar and an extra day every fourth year, leap year.

The Julian calendar was a temporary solution to the calendar drift problem. While it was much more accurate than the old Roman calendar, it was not precise enough to avoid problems in future centuries. The Julian year, of 365¼ days, was eleven minutes and forty-six seconds longer than the true solar year. This created an error of about a day for every 128 years.

Dates slowly began to lose correlation with the seasons and the sun again. The vernal equinox (March 21) was used to fix the date of Easter, but by 1582, it had drifted to March 11 on the Julian calendar. In that year Pope Gregory XIII reformed the calendar again, proclaiming that October 15 would be the day following October 4, 1582. Many people were greatly upset by the ten "lost" days. Employees demanded a full month's pay for October and others actually thought that they had lost ten days of their life! The leap year was also readjusted to eliminate the discrepancy. The Gregorian calendar omitted leap year from years that ended in hundreds, unless they were divisible by four hundred. It also firmly established January 1 as the first day of the year, even though it had a pagan origin. This is the calendar we use today.

Because the Gregorian reform came from Rome, Protestants refused to recognize it. England did not accept the Gregorian calendar until 1752. The Old English new year began on March 25. With the Gregorian calendar it switched to January 1.

The Jewish calendar operates on a lunar year. Each month starts with a new moon, and an extra month (Jewish leap year) is added each year to keep in step with the seasons. Easter is tied to Passover and thus to the lunar year. Easter is set as the first Sunday after the first full moon that comes on or after March 21, and if the full moon happens to fall on a Sunday, the following Sunday is Easter. Simple enough!

Other cultures operate on a lunar calendar. In Islam the year is 354 or 355 days long, as decreed by the Koran. The new month doesn't begin until the new moon is actually seen. Therefore, it can vary from place to place, depending upon weather conditions. Many Muslim countries have crescent moons on their flags. Because the Muslim months are out of step with the solar year, they have absolutely no relation to the seasons and can occur at any time throughout the year.

The Romans dated their years from the founding of Rome, by Remus and Romulus, in 753 B.C., and their practice was followed by the Christian world until A.D. 527, when an abbot suggested dating years starting with the birth of Christ. However, the abbot, Dionysius Exiguus, miscalculated the year in which Christ was born, and the error was never corrected. Christ was probably born in about 4 B.C. This system wasn't fully accepted until A.D. 816.

What is a "Texas leaguer" in baseball?

A Texas leaguer is a blooper, or a softly hit ball, that drops just over the head of an infielder and just in front of the outfielders. This type of hit is known as a Texas leaguer because, back in 1886, Toledo was able to beat Syracuse on the strength of several bloop singles that were hit by three players who had just been called up to the majors from the Texas minor league.

Why do the "Dutch" wear wooden shoes?

The Netherlands is one of the Low Countries, so named because much of its land is below sea level or is comprised of wetlands. (They say the Netherlands is so flat, that if you stand on a chair, you can see clear across the whole country!) The Nederlanders have reclaimed much land from the sea through the construction of dikes and windmills. Their famous windmills have been used since the early sixteenth century to pump water out of the wet areas into canals and create more land for agriculture. Dikes were built to keep the sea at bay and prevent flooding.

Since much of the Netherlands' coastal land was soggy, special shoes were needed to work the fields. Rubber boots weren't available, so the Dutch took to wearing "sabots" or wooden shoes. Such shoes, made from beech or chestnut wood, are water resistant and perfect for walking in the wetlands.

While wooden shoes and windmills are not used much anymore, they will always be a symbol of the Netherlands' battle with the sea and are great tourist attractions.

Why is there a seventh-inning stretch at baseball games?

Baseball is supposed to be America's national pastime. However, at times it can be a tedious and boring affair. There are some people who equate sitting through a game with watching paint dry. Perhaps it is for these people that the seventh-inning stretch was started.

There are two theories behind its origin. The more interesting and less believable one is that President William Howard Taft attended a Washington Senators game during his term in office. Halfway through the seventh inning he had to leave the game. As he rose to leave, all the spectators, out of respect for his office, also rose while he left the stadium. This is believable enough, though why fans would have done this at later games doesn't make sense. If the President had sneezed during the seventh inning, would we all be saying a seventh inning "bless you" today? Probably not!

The more accepted theory credits its beginning to an 1882 baseball game at Manhattan College in New York City. The Manhattan coach, Brother Jasper, noticing how restless the student fans were, asked them to stand up and stretch during the seventh inning. This practice became standard at subsequent Manhattan College games. When the college team played some exhibition games at the Polo Grounds against the New York Giants, the students did their seventh inning stretch, and thus it started to catch on at the major league level.

Was there ever a real "Uncle Ben"?

Yes. The original Uncle Ben was a black rice farmer who lived in Texas. His rice crop was renowned among the rice millers in and around Houston for being of the highest quality. His rice was so good that the other farmers proudly compared their rice to his, claiming it was "as good as Uncle Ben's."

In the late 1940s two of the founders of Converted Rice, Inc. (forerunner of Uncle Ben's, Inc.) were having dinner in their favorite Chicago restaurant, discussing how to better market their "converted" rice in the United States. They both were familiar with the Uncle Ben quality story and decided to call their product Uncle Ben's Converted Brand Rice and manufacture it in the rice-growing area around Houston, where Uncle Ben was said to have farmed.

The restaurant's maître d', Frank Brown, was a close friend of the two men. They talked him into posing for the famous Uncle Ben portrait that is still on the company's boxes today.

Why do fireflies light up?

Fireflies or lightning bugs are beetles that are able to produce light chemically. This phenomenon is called bioluminescence. They are usually seen flashing their "taillights" during the summer in the early evening. Most U.S. species are found east of the Rockies. Their light can be in shades of yellow, green, or red, depending on the species. (The Paraguayan railway beetle has both green and red lights, like a railroad lantern.) Flashing is a form of sexual communication be-

tween males and females seeking mates. The male's light is twice as bright as the female's.

If you have ever noticed, some fireflies flash while they are moving upward though the air. These are the males strutting their stuff. The females can be found hiding in the grass or bushes, giving off their dimmer flashes to attract the flying males. Different species flash at different rates to ensure that a mate of the same species answers.

In the eastern United States, the most common species of firefly is *Photinus pyralis*. The male of this species flashes at intervals of six seconds and the female responds about two seconds later. One clever insect, the female *Photuris pennsylvanica* firefly, lures the males of other species by flashing the male's light pattern, and then devours him!

The firefly's light organ is found in the abdomen. The light is chemically created. ATP (adenosine triphosphate) supplies the energy for the light-producing reaction between luciferin and the enzyme luciferase, which are bound up with magnesium and oxygen in the abdomen. Since abundant oxygen is required, the light organ has numerous trachea (air tubes). When the chemical pyrophosphate is released into the abdomen, the bonds holding the other bound-up chemicals are broken and they are released, creating light. Another chemical released a couple of seconds later turns off the reaction.

Unlike a lightbulb that is hot and loses most of its energy as heat loss, the firefly's light is cool. And, it is about 98 percent energy-efficient. (Well, there's another project for scientists to work on.)

Some people have put the firefly's light to use. For instance, many tropical peoples have developed the practice of putting several in a jar for use as a natural flashlight.

How do certain detergents make "whites whiter," and what is blueing?

Most clothes detergents get your whites clean. However, white fabrics tend to yellow with age. They can be perfectly clean and still appear yellow. To make clothes appear whiter and brighter, manufacturers began adding blueing agents to detergent earlier in the century. Blue tends to absorb yellow light. By adding a very slight blue tinge to whites, the yellow light wavelengths are absorbed instead of reflected, making whites appear less yellow and therefore whiter.

More recently, optical brighteners have replaced blueing. Optical brighteners absorb ultraviolet light and change it to blue light. The blue light helps to cancel out the yellow light, making whites whiter. While your clothes will indeed look whiter, they may in fact appear to be slightly bluer. Now, if they could only find a way to add optical brighteners to toothpaste!

Why are the British referred to as "limeys"?

During the sixteenth, seventeenth, and eighteenth centuries, the greatest killer at sea was not sharks or pirates or ship-wrecks, but scurvy. On Vasco de Gama's historic first trip around Africa's Cape of Good Hope, scurvy killed some one hundred of his one hundred and seventy men. Scurvy results from the lack of ascorbic acid in the diet. The symptoms of scurvy are swollen, bleeding gums, hard patches of skin, easy bruising, stiffness of the joints, weakness, and then finally death. Vitamin C, which contains ascorbic acid, gives imme-diate relief from these symptoms.

It takes six weeks on a diet without vitamin C to cause scurvy, so it wasn't a problem at sea until very long voyages were undertaken. Columbus had no scurvy problems on his voyages to the New World because he was never at sea over six weeks at a time. The British navy spent long stretches of time at sea acquiring and keeping their large empire. The typical British sailor's weekly diet, between 1622 and 1825, consisted of the following: 7 gallons of beer, 4 pounds of salt beef, 2 pounds of salt pork, 12 ounces of cheese, 6 ounces of butter, 3 pints of oatmeal, and 2 pints of dried peas. This diet contained no vitamin C at all.

In 1753, Scottish naval surgeon James Lind recommended adding lemon juice to the sailor's diet to prevent and cure scurvy. The British felt this was too expensive and did not act on his advice for another forty years. By 1795, lemon juice consumption on board ships was compulsory and scurvy was eradicated, only to return in the nineteenth century when the navy switched to lime juice, which has a lower ascorbic acid content.

The British navy was the only navy that used lime juice, which seemed unusual to sailors from other countries. Other navies supplied their sailors with lemons or oranges. To poke fun at the British sailors, Americans and Australians referred to them as "limeys." This derogatory term was later broadened to include anyone from England. Today, however, the British no longer take offense at the term.

Why do trains have a caboose?

The first caboose on record is attributed to conductor Nat Williams of the Auburn and Syracuse Railroad. In the 1840s he converted a small boxcar by cutting a hole in its roof and perching himself upon crates so he could watch the train ahead. He furnished it with a wooden box for a seat and a large barrel for a table. He also outfitted it with such emergency supplies as tools, chains, flags, and lanterns. By the latter half of the nineteenth century, cabooses were standardized, having three or four bunks for the crew, a stove, counter, desk, and chairs.

The most distinctive feature of modern cabooses, aside from their red color, is the cupola or observation tower, which is reached by steel ladders. The tower has seats and windows that allow observation in all directions. Observation of the cars was important in the old days. The wheels could heat up and smoke, causing danger to the train. Before the advent of air brakes, the crew had to walk along the top of the train, from car to car, to adjust the small steel wheels that controlled each car's brakes. The caboose served as a mobile office, living quarters, and kitchen for the "running crew," which included the conductor and four or five brakemen. Hence the name "caboose," which derives from the Dutch "kombias," meaning a ship's galley.

Cabooses were probably painted red so that the engineer in the locomotive could easily see where the end of the train was. The conductor could also communicate with the engineer from the caboose via radio and hand signals.

Modern trains have computer-monitored brakes and there is no longer a need for watching the train or walking along the tops of the cars. Today, train crews consist of two or three people, all of whom ride in the cab of the engine. Now you are more likely to see a caboose attached to a restaurant than to a train. The age of the caboose is past.

Why does your skin wrinkle after a long bath?

After a long bath or a refreshing swim, you will probably emerge with clammy, wrinkled skin. Under normal circumstances the skin is water-resistant, but prolonged immersion in water changes this. The skin has a protective barrier made up of the protein keratin. Keratin is manufactured by cells in the epidermis to block out moisture, bacteria, and other foreign matter.

Prolonged exposure to water causes the cells in the epidermal layer to absorb water and swell. The enlarged cells cause the skin to pucker and wrinkle. Several minutes after toweling off, the water in the skin cells evaporates and the cells return to their normal shape and size. Otherwise, we would all be walking around looking like California raisins.

Where did the golf terms "bogey" and "birdie" come from?

Bogey is another one of those weird terms common to the game of golf. When a player completes a hole in one stroke over par, it is called a bogey. The term derives from an old song called "Colonel Bogey." For some unknown reason it became popular in England for Colonel Bogey's name to be used in reference to any player who could complete a hole in the least number of strokes. American golfers were accustomed to using the word "par" and used the word "bogey" for one *over* par. If you are lucky or talented enough to complete a hole of golf at one stroke under par, this is called a birdie.

While golf and many of its traditions originated in Scotland, the term "birdie" has an American origin. The story goes that the term was first coined by a golfer at the Atlantic City Country Club in the early 1900s. After completing a par four hole in three shots he remarked what a "bird" it was. At that time, "bird" was a slang term for a rarity.

Why can your car radio receive FM stations in a tunnel but not AM stations?

AM (amplitude modulation) signals are transmitted at low frequencies ranging from 540 to 1600 kilohertz (540,000 to 1,600,000 cycles per second). These signals have wavelengths of two hundred to five hundred meters.

FM (frequency modulation) radio signals are transmitted at higher frequencies of from 88 to 108 megahertz (88,000,000 to 108,000,000 cycles per second). These signals have wavelengths of only a few meters.

The much shorter wavelengths of FM signals are not as easily absorbed by objects as are the longer AM waves. Instead of being absorbed by objects, FM waves are reflected and scattered about. This is why television signals are sent at wavelengths a little greater than and a little less than FM bands. In fact, FM radio signals are found right between those of television channels 6 and 7.

Why do we celebrate Halloween?

The origins of Halloween are very old and very strange. Long before the Christian era, the Druids of Great Britain used to celebrate the festival of Samhain (summers end), practicing mystical rites and ceremonies.

November 1 was the first day of the Druid year and the festival of their sun god. They celebrated the day by lighting fires. They believed that on the eve of the new year, the god of death summoned all the souls of the dead who had died during that year and decided what animal form their spirits would take when they came back to life. They thought that the souls of the good would return as humans and that the punishment for the evil could be lessened by praying and the offering of gifts to the god of death. Cats were sacred to the druids, as they were thought to contain the wicked souls of the dead.

Later, under Roman rule, aspects of the Roman pagan harvest festival of Pomona were added. In the seventh century Pope Boniface IV recognized the day of the festival, November 1, and the night before, giving it the name All Hallows' or All Saints' Day, thereby making it into a celebration of all Catholic saints.

The practice of carving a pumpkin into a jack-o'-lantern can be traced back to the Druids. It seems a man named Jack was banned from heaven because he was too stingy and was not allowed into hell because he played pranks on the devil. He was therefore condemned to wander the earth in limbo with a lantern, waiting for Judgment Day. Children in Scotland carved turnips into jack-o'-lanterns with candles placed inside. Scottish immigrants to America found the native pumpkin was more suitable for carving.

It was also believed that on the eve of All Hallows' Day, ghosts and witches were most likely to roam about. Therefore, the custom of wearing costumes to fool evil spirits was practiced. The prevalent belief of the time about witches has carried over to the Pennsylvania Dutch of today. They paint hex signs on their barns to ward off evil spirits and bring good luck. Another American belief was that iron could ward off witches, especially if it was formed into the shape of a horseshoe. Horseshoes are still considered signs of good luck, but only if they are hung with the ends pointing upward. If the ends point down, the magical powers run out.

Our modern custom of trick-or-treating is from seventeenth-century Ireland. The Irish poor of the time would go from door to door asking for money to buy food for a feast in honor of St. Columba, who had taken the place of Samhain, the old god of the dead. St. Columba was a sixth-century monk who had converted the Picts to Christianity. The Gaels also had the practice of giving cakes, called soul cakes, to the poor at Samhain in return for their prayers for a good harvest. A more recent influence may have been Plough Day in England. Ploughmen would go begging from door to door and if turned away would threaten to plough up the stingy farmer's crops. Some or all of these practices helped result in today's custom of trick or treating.

We can thank Irish immigrants for bringing over the pre-Halloween custom known as "mischief night." Usually "observed" the night before Halloween, it involved boys and young men playing tiresome pranks on people or committing acts of vandalism. Today, rubbing soap on windows, throwing eggs at houses and cars, and putting toilet paper in trees are favorite activities. But there appears to be no real underlying meaning or purpose to these tricks.

Why do pigeons like statues and high ledges?

You may have asked yourself this question if you've ever been stuck under a highway overpass at rush hour. Pigeons love to roost on high, hard ledges and objects like statues.

Pigeons are not native to the United States, but like many of us, emigrated from Europe. They are members of the dove family, as their other name, rockdove, suggests, and are native to the rocky sea cliffs of the northern Atlantic Ocean and Mediterranean Sea. This may explain their penchant for living among the skyscrapers of our metropolitan areas. Since being introduced into the United States, they have spread to all of the lower forty-eight states and thrive on a diet of wild seeds.

Pigeons were domesticated thousands of years ago as couriers. They can fly at speeds of up to eighty miles per hour and find their way back home after traveling hundreds of miles. Our urban pigeons are the half-wild descendants of these domesticated birds. This is why they show no fear of man and gladly take handouts and scavenge the garbage for pizza crusts. Through our kindness we have helped these "rats on the wing" to become highly successful city dwellers. In some cities, there are so many pigeons that their dried droppings can create a dust that can cause respiratory irritation when inhaled.

Another bird introduced from Europe is the starling. In 1890, a flock of starlings were released in New York City's

Central Park. This aggressive species quickly spread throughout the entire continental United States and southern Canada, displacing several native species along the way. While they are generally considered a nuisance bird by many, they have proven to be very effective at insect pest control.

Did you ever hear of the "State of Franklin"?

The State of Franklin was a short-lived government that existed between 1784 and 1788, in what is now eastern Tennessee. North Carolina ceded its western territory to the federal government in 1784. Congress acted too slowly in accepting the offer and it was therefore withdrawn. However, the area was left in limbo, with no government or federal protection. So its inhabitants formed their own "state" and named it Franklin, in hopes of gaining the support of Benjamin Franklin. They made Greenville their capital and elected John Sevier as their governor. There was no "state" currency, so officials had to be paid in furs, tobacco, and whiskey.

Unable to gain the recognition of Congress or Benjamin Franklin, they rejoined North Carolina in 1788, and were again ceded to the federal government. The region became part of eastern Tennessee in 1796. John Sevier was subsequently elected first governor of Tennessee.

Why do pregnant women crave pickles?

The seemingly irrational cravings of a pregnant woman in fact turn out to be very logical and practical. It is the body's way of asking for certain nutrients in which it may be deficient. In the case of pickles, it is the salt that the body really is craving. Women have been told for years to reduce salt intake, but a pregnant woman needs a lot more salt than she normally would. A woman needs to make about 40 percent more blood to feed the placenta while pregnant. Salt is a key ingredient in maintaining this higher blood level. The fetus needs a lot of salt, too. The unborn baby is constantly bathed in a saline solution. All this extra salt has to come from somewhere. By craving things such as pickles, pretzels, and anchovies, the body is assured of getting enough salt.

Why some pregnant women put pickles in their ice cream is another story.

Why are marathons 26 miles, 385 yards long?

Twenty-six miles, 385 yards is a rather odd distance for a foot race. Most other running races are measured in lengths of even numbers. The marathon, however, has an ancient history, going back to the early Greek Olympics.

The Greeks started the Olympics in 776 B.C. to honor the god Zeus. Held every four years, they brought together athletes from all the Greek cities. A nationwide truce was called for the five days of competition held in Olympia. The first day was devoted to ceremonies, banquets, and sacrifices. Early events included running, boxing, wrestling, pentathalon, and various horse and chariot races.

After 490 B.C., a special long-distance race, the marathon, was added to commemorate the legendary feat of a Greek soldier. It was said that he ran from the Plain of Marathon to Athens, a distance of 22 miles, 1,470 yards, to bring the news of the Greek victory over the Persian army. Upon exclaiming "Rejoice! We have won!," he collapsed and died.

The Greek Olympic marathon was a distance of about 25 miles, and was run by young men in the nude.

The games were abolished in A.D. 393 by Roman emperor Theodosius I after Greece lost its independence.

The Olympic Games were revived in Athens in 1896 by a Frenchman, Baron Pierre de Coubertin. The first few modern Olympiads had marathons of varying lengths. It wasn't until the 1908 games, in London, that today's distance was first instituted. The British Olympic Committee decided to have the race start at the royal residence at Windsor Castle and end in front of the royal box in the stadium in London, a distance of 26 miles, 385 yards. This distance was standardized at the 1924 Olympic Games and has been used ever since.

Today, all marathons, including non-Olympic races, are kept at this odd distance and all competitors are encouraged to wear clothing!

Do microwaves really cook food from the inside out?

Microwaves are a form of electromagnetic radiation that have shorter wavelengths than television signals but longer wavelengths than visible light. One curious property of microwaves is their ability to excite or agitate water molecules but not other molecules. The reason for this is that water molecules have a positive end (hydrogen) and a negative end (oxygen). Most other types of molecules are neutral. Microwaves act like little magnets, attracting and repelling the positive and negative ends alternately, thus causing water molecules to spin. Microwave radiation alternates its field 2,400,000,000 times per second, spinning the water molecules incredibly fast. All this spinning of molecules creates a great deal of friction, and friction causes heat.

The ability of microwaves to cook food was accidentally discovered by Percy LeBaron Spencer of the Raytheon Company in the 1940s when he found that they melted a candy bar he had in his pocket.

Most foods are made up of molecules of carbohydrate, fat, and protein. Interspersed among the food molecules are water molecules. The spinning water molecules heat up the surrounding molecules and cook the food.

Conventional ovens heat up the air that surrounds the outer layers of food. The heated outer layers gradually transfer the heat to the inner layers of food, cooking it from the outside in. In microwave cooking all the food molecules are heated at approximately the same time. However, since the air inside the microwave oven remains cool, the outer layers of food during cooking may be cooler than the inner layers, due to heat loss to the air. This gives the impression that the inside has cooked first.

One common complaint about microwave cooking is that bread products come out soggy, not crisp. This is because in microwaves, the heated water molecules rise quickly to the surface of the food, condensing into water droplets on the surface. This results in soggy bread. In conventional ovens, the heated water vapor rises more slowly and then evaporates rather than condensing when it hits the hot, dry oven air. As a result, bread will be crisp on the outside and moist on the inside, where some water remains, unless the bread is overcooked.

Why do we give names to hurricanes?

The world is a big place and at any one time there can be more than one tropical storm or hurricane brewing. Obviously, it is important that the folks reporting storms from around the world have accurate data.

In order to reduce the chance of confusing one storm with another, meteorologists decided to give each reported hurricane its own name. Before that they were referred to by their latitude and longitude positions, which were constantly changing. Names are easier to remember and less boring than simply assigning numbers.

Since hurricanes were first reported via radio, during World War II, the names they were given were from the phonetic alphabet—Abel, Baker, Charlie, etc. Later, in 1953, hurricanes began being named after women, much to the later chagrin of the feminists! In 1979, the World Meteorological Association began using both women's and men's names, so as not to slight either gender. Hurricane names are now assigned alphabetically at the beginning of the year, alternating between male and female names.

Every five or six years the names are recycled and used again. However, a storm of great notoriety, such as Andrew, which ravaged southern Florida in 1992, has had its name retired. Andrew was last used in 1986, for a tropical depression that left 300,000 homeless in Jamaica and Haiti.

Why do champagne bottles have that deep indentation at the bottom?

The deep indentation at the bottom of champagne bottles is there for a practical purpose, not just to cheat you out of a little of the bubbly. There are three main reasons for the indentation (referred to as the "punt"). The first relates to traditional design. It was found that a recessed cavity in the bottom made pouring from the bottle much easier, especially for people with small hands. Also, when you hold the bottle by the bottom lip, the warmth of your hands does not raise the temperature of the chilled champagne.

The second reason has to do with the history of winemaking. Historically, champagne bottles were stored horizontally for fermentation and aging. By laying the bottles end to end, with the top of one bottle inserted into the punt of another, more bottles could be stored per bin.

The third reason has to do with the structural integrity of the bottle. Champagne is under pressure in the bottle. (Hence the warning labels instructing you to aim the bottle away from people when opening. One champagne cork was shot a record distance of 109$^{1}/_{2}$ feet, upon opening!) By having the indentation in the lower portion of the bottle, the glass is made structurally stronger.

Next time you pour from a bottle of champagne for your friends, do it by holding the lip of the punt between thumb and forefinger. If you really want to impress them, tell them why the dent is there.

How are interstate highways numbered in the United States?

Believe it or not, this is one government practice that is organized and logical. All east-west interstate highways are even-numbered and increase from south to north. Thus, east-west Interstate 80 is north of I-70. North-south interstates are odd-numbered and increase from west to east. City bypasses and spurs have triple digits and are numbered odd or even depending on their directional orientation.

When did it first become offensive to extend the middle finger?

Thrusting out the middle finger or "flipping the bird" is one of the more familiar hand gestures. Its popularity is worldwide and it has been around a very long time. No one is sure how it originated but we know the Romans used it at the time of Christ.

While the meaning of "the finger" is understood around the world, there are several gestures that are peculiar to different regions.

In most of Europe the V sign is meant to represent victory when the palm is kept facing away from you, as was popularized by Winston Churchill during World War II. However, in England and Australia, when the palm faces in, the V sign means "shove it." Former President George Bush made the embarrassing gaffe of flashing the "shove it" sign to the people of Australia during his 1992 visit there, much to the amusement of the Aussies. The President didn't know that there are two ways to give the V sign, or maybe he just forgot. Either way, it was not much of a victory for George "down under."

The American OK sign is widely accepted as meaning all right. In Brazil, however, it is considered obscene. It is also considered impolite in Russia and Greece. In Colombia, the

OK sign is placed over the nose to imply that a person is a homosexual.

Tapping the ends of the index fingers together, in Egypt, indicates that two people are sleeping together. It can also be used to ask another person to sleep with you. Slapping the back of the fist with the palm means "----you" in Italy and Chile. The same message can be conveyed in the Mediterranean by hitting the biceps and lifting the forearm.

In Taiwan, blinking of the eyes is considered impolite. In Italy, flicking the ear with the finger signifies that the man in question is effeminate.

Just as there are many gestures in the world to convey one's negative feelings about another, there are also regional differences to show approval. Men around the world have several gestures to imply that a woman is pretty. In the United States, men lift their eyebrows, in the Arab world a man grabs his beard, while in Greece he would stroke his cheek. In Italy, a man sticks his finger into his cheek and rotates it, Frenchmen kiss their fingertips, and Brazilians will pretend to hold up a telescope to their eye.

Obviously, almost any gesture can have meaning, either positive or negative, somewhere in the world. So next time you travel abroad, be careful how you gesture with your hands, you might unwittingly attract unwanted attention from the natives.

Why do roses have thorns?

Roses, technically speaking, have prickles, not thorns. Thorns are botanically considered to be modified branches, like those found on the hawthorn. Prickles are actually outgrowths of the outer skin of the stem. Prickles easily break off from the stem; thorns are hard to break off because they are part of the woody tissue of the plant.

Both thorns and prickles serve to protect the plant from

being eaten. Most plant eaters would rather do without a mouthful of cuts, so they look for an easier meal elsewhere.

Why is a frankfurter called a hot dog?

You may have guessed this one. Around the turn of the century, it was thought that frankfurters were actually made from dog parts. Yuck!

At that time, a concessionaire at New York's Polo Grounds named Harry Stevens had his vendors yell "Get your red-hot dachshund sausages!" The famous sports cartoonist T. A. Dorgan liked this expression and took to calling them hot dogs. In 1900, as a joke, he drew a frankfurter shaped like a dachshund inside a bun. A new expression was born.

Today the words hot dog, frankfurter, and weiner all are synonymous. The name frankfurter derives from a coarsely ground, highly seasoned sausage that was popular in Frankfurt, Germany. The word weiner has its origins in a less seasoned, finer ground sausage common in Vienna, Austria. A Bavarian, Antoine Feuchtwanger, brought the frank idea to America in the 1880s, selling them in St. Louis, Missouri. They were sold hot and were hard to handle, so Feuchtwanger enlisted his brother-in-law, a baker, to create an elongated bun to hold the hot franks.

Today, neither Frankfurt or Vienna want to take credit for the hot dog. Apparently, they consider their own local cuisines to be above association with this American favorite.

What exactly is "dry beer"?

"Dry" beers are similar to dry wines, in that they are not sweet in taste. Dry beer also leaves little aftertaste. The "dry brew" method of brewing is a longer, natural process, in which more of the malt and grains are converted to fermentable sugars. The sugars interact with yeast and the subsequent fermentation process produces a beer with the unique dry taste.

In Japan, where the first dry beer was brewed by Asahi, most dry beers contain about 10 percent more alcohol than regular beers. American dry beers have no increased alcohol content.

With the world population exploding, when will we run out of space?

As of 1990, the total estimated world population was 5,333,000,000. Sounds like quite a few people. Estimates for the world population in the year 2025 go up to 8,177,100,000! At this rate, will we run out of land and have chronic overcrowding?

Actually there is plenty of space for everyone on Earth. The total land mass of the earth is 57,900,000 square miles. If we were to spread the 1990 world population evenly around the earth, each person would have a roomy six and a half acres to call his/her own. If you could take the 1990 world population and crowd everyone together, allowing a two-foot-by-two-foot square for each to stand in, you could fit everyone into an area slightly larger than Jacksonville, Florida. Now that would be a lot of retirees! In an "overcrowded" city like New York, which has a population density of 23,494 per square mile, each person would have a spacious 1,187 square feet if evenly distributed.

Even if the world population increases by 65 percent by the year 2025, as projected, that would still leave each of us four and a half acres to roam.

Of course this example is silly. Much of the world's land is not really habitable. The point is made, however, that we will not run out of living space in the foreseeable future. The real problem facing us is the depletion of our resources, such as food, energy, rain forests, clean air, and water.

Why do we yell "Geronimo!" when we jump out of planes?

Well, we don't all jump out of planes or there would be a lot more yelling going on, and not necessarily Geronimo! Believe it or not, this expression does go back to the time of Geronimo, the great Native American leader, who is first credited with its use. Legend has it that while being pursued by the U.S. Cavalry near Medicine Bluffs, Oklahoma, the Apache chief was trapped at the edge of a cliff. Rather than surrender, he leapt off the cliff on horseback, yelling out his name, "Geronimo!" to taunt the troops. He survived this jump and rode away to a short-lived freedom. He was eventually captured and died while a prisoner at Fort Sill, Oklahoma, in 1909.

During World War II the paratroopers in the 82nd Airborne Division, at Fort Bragg, North Carolina, having heard of the legend, began shouting "Geronimo!" as they jumped from their planes. Had a different Native American chief ridden his horse off a cliff, parachutists might very well be shouting "Crazy Horse" today when they jump out of planes. They would be half right, anyway.

Geronimo wasn't always a ferocious warrior. As a matter of fact his given name was "Goyahkla," Native American for "one who yawns." It wasn't until the Mexican army killed his family that he began to hate all of them. The Mexicans gave him the name Geronimo, after St. Jerome, whom they pleaded with for help after a particularly bloody battle with the seemingly invincible Native American.

Why do spokes on a wagon wheel appear to move backward on television or movie screens?

This phenomenon has nothing to do with the mind playing tricks on you or weird physics. It is simply an optical illusion created by the movie film. When you watch a movie, as you are probably aware, you are not watching a continuous flow of action, but rather a series of still shots run at twenty-four frames per second. The human eye cannot detect the gaps between each frame because they occur so rapidly. We see a smooth-running movie.

However, the gaps in the film do have an interesting effect on spinning objects, such as wagon wheels. If the spokes were spinning at the same rate as the frames of the movie, twenty-four per second, then the spokes would have returned to exactly the same position for every frame and the wheels would appear to be stationary. When the spokes are spinning at a little less than the speed of the film, they don't make it all the way back to their original position, and are a little further behind on each frame. As consecutive frames are rolled, the spokes gradually appear to move backward. This illusion is also evident on television, which flashes the picture at thirty times per second.

So the illusion is on the film itself, and your eyes are correctly seeing what is actually on the film.

If you ever watch a wagon wheel, or some similar spinning object in real life, you will not observe this effect. If you do, maybe you have watched too many Westerns on the tube.

Why doesn't the North Star ever appear to move in the sky as other stars do?

Sailors have used the North Star (Polaris) since early times to navigate, since it remains in a relatively fixed location in the northern sky. If you view Polaris from various points around the Northern Hemisphere, you will be facing almost due north. Actually, all stars are set in a fixed position in the sky relative to each other. It is the movement of the Earth, rotating on its axis, that makes the stars, including the sun, appear to move across the sky. (Planets, however, do move on their own through the sky and can thus be differentiated from stars.)

The North Star is situated directly above the northern axis of Earth. Thus, as Earth spins, Polaris, on the northern pivot point of rotation, does not appear to move from its polar position. Hence the name Polaris.

Over the millennia, all the stars are shifting in relation to Earth, due to a phenomenon known as precession. The direction that Earth's axis is pointing is slowly, almost imperceptibly, changing, in much the same way that a spinning top leans one way and then another. This precession occurs because Earth is not a perfect sphere, but is about twenty-seven miles wider in diameter at the equator than between the poles. The bulge in the middle is caused by Earth's rotation. Earth's slow wobble traces out a circular pattern in the sky, and it takes twenty-six thousand years to complete one circle. For this reason, Polaris will not always be the "North" Star. In about fifteen thousand years, the star Vega will take the place of Polaris in the northern sky. By A.D. 27,990, Polaris will return to its present position as the North Star.

It is easy to find the North Star. Locate the Big Dipper. Form a line between the two pointer stars, follow it north to Polaris, as illustrated above.

Who invented the first condom?

Condoms have been with us much longer than you might have imagined. Condoms are supposedly named after the apocryphal "Dr. Condom," or Conton, who is supposed to have made them for Charles II, out of lamb's intestines, which were dried and then well oiled. The male sheath, however, had been around long before the time of Charles II.

Before the time of Christ, the Chinese made them with oiled silk paper (the first lubricated condom!). It is rumored that Roman soldiers would make condoms from the muscle tissue of their defeated foes. By medieval times, the spread of syphilis increased the use of condoms greatly.

In the 1800s condoms were made from animal intestines that were soaked in an alkaline solution, scraped, disinfected with the vapor of burning brimstone, washed, inflated, dried, cut to approximately seven inches, and fitted with a ribbon on the open end. The Catholic Church wasn't too crazy about this prophylactic profusion and in 1826 Pope Leo XIII condemned their use. Despite the objections of his holiness, condoms were here to stay!

Why is a boxing "ring" square?

Boxing matches weren't always fought in a roped-off ring (really a square). The sport of boxing dates back to the Greek Olympic games of 688 B.C., and is probably much older. Far from being in a ring, the ancient Greek fighters remained seated, face-to-face, and pummeled each other until one or the other was knocked unconscious. Primitive indeed!

The bloodthirsty Romans made boxing a little more interesting by allowing the combatants to wear brass knuckles and, later, to use spiked clubs. Because of the increased violence, and to make the "sport" more interesting, the Romans allowed the men to fight standing up within a circular area instead of sitting down. So many fighters died, however, that even the Romans found it too uncivilized and banned boxing around 30 B.C.

The sport was revived in England in the early 1700s by James Figg, a fencer who applied some fencing principles to boxing. Early-eighteenth-century boxers would fight, barefisted, in the open air with a crowd of spectators forming a loose circle or "ring" around them. No rest periods were allowed.

In the 1840s boxing rules started to become standardized with the use of the London Prize Ring Rules. Matches were broken up into rounds, with a round ending whenever one man was knocked down. The next round would begin within thirty seconds, if the participants were still able to stand up.

Fights could go on for hours and last seventy or eighty rounds! Boxing, however, was still considered barbaric and was outlawed in England by the middle of the nineteenth century.

With the introduction of the Marquis of Queensbury Rules, the sport became more standardized and was generally tolerated by the British police, even though it was not entirely legal. The practice of fighting within a roped-off square became common, but the term "ring" was still employed. The Queensbury Rules also encouraged the use of gloves and established rounds of three minutes in length, with a one-minute break in between.

The Queensbury Rules were written in 1867 by a man named John Graham Chambers, not by the Marquis of Queensbury, although the Marquis did endorse and sponsor their use.

The word boxing, by the way, has nothing to do with the boxlike shape of the wooden ring. It is derived from the Middle English word for slap or strike—box. In England, thrashing someone is still referred to as "boxing their ears."

Who was the first European to "discover" the New World?

No it wasn't Christopher Columbus, Leif Eriksson, or Erik the Red. According to the *Book of Flatey,* a collection of Icelandic stories compiled in the 1300s, it was a Norse trader named Bjarni Herjulfsson. Supposedly, Herjulfsson was blown off course in A.D. 986 on his way from Iceland to Greenland. He sighted what is now believed to be Cape Cod. As he was behind schedule and also not very curious, he did not land. Instead, he traveled northeast toward Greenland, possibly sighting Nova Scotia and Newfoundland along the way.

It wasn't until fourteen years later, in A.D. 1000 that Viking Leif Eriksson landed in Newfoundland. Leif was the son of

Erik Thorvaldson, also known as Erik the Red. Erik's father had been exiled from Norway to Iceland for having committed murder, when Erik was ten years old. After his father died, Erik became involved in several killings and was expelled from Iceland for three years, in approximately A.D. 985. With nowhere else to go, Erik and a group of his supporters sailed west to find a land rumored to have been sighted by another Norwegian, Gunnbjorn Ulfsson, around A.D. 900. They made landfall on an ice-covered island and settled on one of the few grassy areas along the coast. Erik decided to turn land promoter and persuaded Icelanders to settle in the new land, which he misleadingly called Greenland.

In the year A.D. 1000, having heard of Bjarni's sightings, Erik's son Leif sailed west once again, landing in Newfoundland. He then sailed south to land in Nova Scotia, and then in Cape Cod, where he and his men spent the winter. The discovery of grapes on the Cape prompted Leif to name this new land Vinland (land of wine). Upon his return home he encouraged other Vikings to colonize this New World. Legend has it that the Vikings explored all along the East Coast of the United States.

The Vikings established a short-lived colony on Newfoundland. For about fifteen years people from Greenland sailed to the new colony. Native Indians are said to have attacked and killed several Norse settlers, including Eriksson's brother Thorwald. Probably because of this, the settlers returned to Greenland, never to visit the New World again. One wonders, how much better could things have been in Greenland?

Was there really ever a Mother Goose?

The collection of nursery rhymes known as *Mother Goose Melodies* allegedly was based on the stories of an actual woman named Goose. Her full name was Elizabeth (Foster)

Goose (or Vergoose). She lived in Massachusetts from 1665 to 1757. Mrs. Goose had ten stepchildren through her marriage to Isaac Goose and had six more of her own, for a total of sixteen children. One of her daughters married Thomas Fleet, a Boston printer. Mrs. Goose told many interesting children's tales, and her son-in-law, Fleet, supposedly printed them in 1719.

This Mother Goose story is an interesting one; unfortunately, it is most probably a fabrication. Most of the songs and rhymes that appeared in *Mother Goose* books actually existed long before they were ever published. They had diverse origins. Several were old English drinking songs, ballads, or satirical pieces. Some were based on actual people or events.

For instance, "Little Jack Horner" is rumored to be a true story. Supposedly, the Bishop of Glastonbury, England, had sent the deeds to twelve properties, baked in a Christmas pie, to King Henry VIII as a gift from the church. Jack Horner, the Bishop's emissary, is said to have lifted the cover of the pie, pulled out a "plum" (one of the deeds), and kept it. The rhyme goes:

> *Little Jack Horner*
> *Sat in a corner.*
> *Eating his Christmas pie.*
> *He put in his thumb*
> *and pulled out a plum,*
> *And said, "What a good boy am I."*

"Jack Spratt" pokes fun at a fat churchman named Archdeacon Pratt. "Sing a Song of Sixpence" recounts the sixteenth-century custom of sealing live birds in a pie to be served at festive occasions. Upon opening, the birds (blackbirds, in this case) would fly out, to the delight of dinner guests.

These early rhymes were obviously for adults. The only published children's tales at the time were lullabies and alphabet rhymes. The Mother Goose stories were popular in France in the mid-1600s.

It wasn't until 1697 that Frenchman Charles Perrault published a collection of these called *History or Tales of Past Times, With Morals.* On the front cover was a picture of an old woman sitting by a fireplace telling stories. On the wall behind her was a sign that read Tales of Mother Goose. The book included "Sleeping Beauty," "Little Red Riding Hood," and "Cinderella."

In 1729, the book was translated into English and published in England with a similar front cover showing the old woman and the sign Mother Goose's Tales. This name was adopted for the title of the book in a 1768 reissue. The book was first published in America in 1786 under the title *Mother Goose's Melody.* With each reissue of the book, new tales and songs were added, including "Humpty Dumpty," "Old King Cole," "Jack and Jill," "Simple Simon," "Hickory

Dickory Dock," etc. The most notable American addition was "Mary Had a Little Lamb."

It wasn't until the mid-1800s that a relative of Elizabeth Goose claimed that she and Fleet had published the songs in 1719. No copies of this work were ever found. While it is true that Mrs. Goose had sixteen grandchildren, it is doubtful that they all lived together in a giant shoe!

What do the initials OK stand for?

OK is not short for Okey-Dokey or any other such nonsense. This universally used expression, meaning all right, is of rather recent American origin. Some linguists maintain that Andrew Jackson first used the expression, having taken it from the Choctaw Indian word "okeh." It was, however, popularized by Martin Van Buren.

Martin Van Buren was president of the United States from 1837 to 1841. Born in Kinderhook, New York, he acquired the friendly nickname "Old Kinderhook." He ran for reelection in 1840 against General William Henry Harrison, who had the snappy nickname "Tippecanoe," referring to this famous victory over the Indians at Tippecanoe. Harrison's running mate was John Tyler, and their campaign slogan was "Tippecanoe and Tyler too!"

During the election campaign, Van Buren was called disparaging nicknames such as "the Little Magician," "King Martin the First," and "the Kinderhook Fox" by his political enemies. His supporters, in an effort to improve the public image of "Old Kinderhook," formed the Democratic OK Club. The expression OK, meaning that Van Buren was all right by the Democrats, quickly spread across the nation, and was one of those slang terms that refused to go away.

"Old Kinderhook" lost the election and is pretty much forgotten by the world today, but his nickname initials are used worldwide. Too bad his campaign platform wasn't as popular as his nickname.

Why is the statuette for the Academy Awards named "Oscar"?

The Academy of Motion Picture Arts and Sciences has been honoring its best with the familiar golden statuette since 1927. In its first few years, the award had no official name. The gold-plated bronze statuette stands ten inches high, weighs seven pounds, and was simply called the "Statuette." The story goes that it acquired its name by chance. A librarian for the academy, Mrs. Margaret Herrick, happened to comment to a reporter that the trophy reminded her of her uncle Oscar Pierce, of Texas. The reporter seized upon this rather mundane comment in his story and it caught on with the public. It must have been a slow news day!

What was the first "four-letter word"?

We all have our favorite "four-letter words." Perhaps your favorite is the f-word, or the d-word, or the s-word. However, none of these is the oldest "four letter word" or the most subject to taboo. The oldest and most socially unacceptable "four-letter word" in history is YHWH! Yes, YHWH! There, the taboo has been broken! Now that you know what it is, you probably can't pronounce it. Well, actually you could. YHWH is the transliteration of the Hebrew word for God, Yahweh (also Yahveh or YHVH). Devout Jews will neither write nor speak the name Yahweh. Many Jews would not even spell out the word God on things such as Bat Mitzvah invitations, instead preferring to omit the o from God—G_D.

Why are people from Indiana called "Hoosiers"?

For over 160 years people from Indiana have been known as "Hoosiers." The curious thing is that no one really seems to know why. All that is known for sure is that the term came into general usage in the 1830s. Even the Indiana State Library doesn't know the origin of the word Hoosier. However, the Indiana Historical Bureau offers the following popular theories:

1. When a visitor hailed a pioneer cabin in Indiana or knocked upon its door, the settler would respond, "Who's yere?" From this frequent response Indiana became the "Who's yere" or Hoosier State. (This explanation sounds kind of lame.)
2. Indiana rivermen were so spectacularly successful in trouncing or "hushing" their adversaries in the brawling that was then common, that they became known as "hushers," eventually Hoosiers.
3. There was once a contractor named Hoosier employed on the Louisville and Portland Canal who preferred to hire laborers from Indiana. They were called "Hoosier's men" and eventually all Indianans were called Hoosiers. This is as good an explanation as any.
4. A theory attributed to Governor Joseph Wright claimed that Hoosier derived from an Indian word for corn, hoosa. Indiana flatboatmen taking corn or maize to New Orleans came to be known as "Hoosa men" or Hoosiers. Unfortunately for this theory, a search of Indian vocabularies by a careful student of linguistics failed to reveal any such word for corn. So much for this explanation.
5. Quite as plausible as any of the above was the facetious explanation offered by author James Whitcomb Riley. He claimed that it originated in the pugnacious habits of our early settlers. They were enthusiastic and vicious fighters who gouged, scratched, and bit off noses and ears. This occurred so often that a settler who came into a tavern the morning after a fight and saw an ear on the floor would touch it with his toe and casually ask, "Whose ear?" This is easily the most ridiculous explanation of them all.

The lack of a reasonable origin or meaning for the name Hoosier has not stopped Indianans from proudly proclaiming that they are Hoosiers, even though they have no idea what a Hoosier is!

Why do we call something that distracts attention from the real issue at hand a "red herring"?

Herring are quite abundant off the coast of northern Europe. They were an important dietary staple. Herring were cured by salting and drying in the sun, causing them to turn brown. When smoked, herring take on a reddish color. Because it preserved so well, sailors favored red herring on long voyages.

Red herring is also very aromatic and had another practical use. Hunters would use this pungent smoke-cured fish to train their hunting dogs to follow a scent. By dragging the fish across the ground, hunters could lay a trail for the dogs to follow. Subsequently, if a hunting dog, tracking game, went off the trail, he was said to be chasing a red herring. It is also said that escaping criminals in the seventeenth century would drag red herring behind them to distract the pursuing bloodhounds from the real trail.

Why are men's underwear also known as BVD's?

BVD is a registered trademark of a company that manufactures men's underwear. The three men who formed the company in 1876 were named Bradley, Voorhies, and Day. Lacking the imagination for a more creative name, they chose their initials—BVD.

Why are rich aristocrats called "blue bloods"?

While we tend to think of blue bloods as being wealthy aristocrats of Western Europe, the name actually originated in Spain. Spain was ruled for over five hundred years by the Moors. They were dark-skinned Islamic warriors who were despised by the native Castilians. The Spanish aristocrats, in order to differentiate themselves from their Morrish rulers, adapted the name "sangreazul" or blue blood. This was a sarcastic reference to the fact that their lighter skin allowed the blue of their veins to show through. The expression later spread to the aristocracy in the rest of Europe.

How does a hot-air balloon steer and stop?

Hot-air ballooning is the most serene and free-spirited way to fly. There is no steering wheel, gas pedal, or brake. Balloons are simple, consisting of a basket, propane burner, and a balloon (the more colorful the better). All the balloon can do on its own is ascend and descend. The rest is up to the wits of its pilot, who, by the way, will always insist that hot-air ballooning is the safest way to fly.

When a balloon lifts off, the pilot really has no idea where

he is going to land. He is at the mercy of the air currents, although he can use them to his best advantage. By ascending and descending, the pilot is able to find different air currents at different heights and utilize them to carry the balloon and its occupants in the desired direction. Balloons, while using the available winds to their advantage, do not perform well under windy conditions. That is why balloons fly only at the hours just before dusk or just after dawn, when the winds are very still.

Well, that explains the basics of steering. Braking, however, is trickier. One way is to time the descent to slowly land in an open area, like a meadow or cornfield. This is the least exciting and safest way to stop.

Another, more radical and gutsy way to slow down is to descend near the treetops and drag the basket along the tops of the trees for a "quickie" stop. If you don't do it right, you could end up with a big hot-air tree fort! The fastest way to stop is to pull the "red line." This is a cord that will quickly release the hot air from the balloon and send it down to the ground.

Ballooning is so unpredictable that ground chase crews must drive after the balloons wherever they go, in order to pick up the crew when they land. Occasionally this is in a farmer's field and some farmers don't take kindly to balloon and chase vehicle knocking down their hard-earned crops of corn, soybeans, or whatever.

The smart balloonist keeps a bottle of spirits in his basket to help soothe any irate farmer's feelings. Speaking of bottles, many balloonists offer romantic evening champagne flights. However, if your pilot starts scraping the treetops, you may feel more nauseous than romantic.

Why aren't typewriter or keyboard keys arranged in alphabetical order?

The first practical typewriter was built in 1867 by Christopher Latham Sholes. E. Remington and Sons, makers of guns in Ilion, New York, put a successful model on the market in 1874. Some early typewriter models had used toy building blocks for keys. These original typewriters did have their keys in more or less alphabetical order, which seemed to make sense at the time. The one little problem with this arrangement was that the early typists became so proficient that the keys would jam up because they typed too fast.

To slow down the typists, the keys were rearranged into a diabolically difficult pattern. Sholes's first typewriter was designed for use with two fingers. Typists learned to use all ten fingers with the rearranged key pattern, which still survives today. The left hand does about 57 percent of the typing, the right only 43 percent. The three weakest and least coordinated fingers, the two pinkies and left ring finger make far more than their share of strokes, and to type the most common words one must move up and down between rows. Even with this difficult key arrangement, some typists are still capable of typing over 170 words per minute on manual typewriters!

You would think, in today's age of word processors and the elimination of carriage bars, that someone would design a more efficient keyboard to speed up productivity and reduce typing fatigue and frustration.

Actually, someone already did. In 1936, August Dvorak researched and designed a more usable keyboard where 70 percent of the typing is done on one row (the home row), 57 percent of the typing done with the right hand, and the stronger fingers do more of the work. Studies showed that the overall finger movement with Dvorak's pattern would be reduced by at least ten times.

Why didn't this wonderful new design catch on? Well, Dvorak had an order to supply the U.S. Navy with two thousand of these typewriters just as World War II was beginning. However, all manufacturers devoted themselves to wartime production and the order was never filled. It never caught on after the conclusion of the war.

Today we have computers and laser printers capable of processing and printing umpteen words per minute but we can't use our twenty-first-century technology to its fullest potential because we cling to a nineteenth-century mentality when it comes to keyboards.

Why do we say "God bless you" after a sneeze?

Why do we bless people when they sneeze? After all, we have no such custom for people when they cough or hiccup. In ancient times, it was believed that the soul left your body when you sneezed and that evil spirits could then enter. Blessing you with the name of God was supposed to prevent this. In the Dark Ages, it was believed that your heart stopped momentarily when you sneezed. You were, in effect, dead for an instant and had to be blessed.

Sneezing is triggered by irritants such as dust, pollen, or pet dander. These particles land on the mucous lining of the nose. The irritation triggers the lungs to inhale, building up high pressure, while the airways are all tightly closed. When the air passages are suddenly opened, the breathing muscle forcibly expels the air, and any irritants, out through the nose and mouth.

Dust and pollen aren't the only things expelled with the air. If you are sick, any viruses in the nasal passages or throat can also be expelled. When you sneeze, mucus-laden air is shot out of your nose and mouth at around one hundred miles per hour. A good blast can travel clear across a room. A sick person could, thus, spread their illness to anyone in the immediate area. Bearing this in mind, perhaps the next time someone sneezes, they should bless *you!*

Why do beer bubbles stream from only certain points in a glass?

All beers have one thing in common, they contain free-floating molecules of carbon dioxide gas (CO_2) in the beer, until the top is removed. The gas collects in the neck of the bottle and exerts a pressure of up to forty-five pounds per square inch. When the cap is removed from a beer bottle, the CO_2 gas rushes outward to equalize the pressure. As it rushes out, the gas is using up kinetic energy from its molecules and this causes an instantaneous drop in the temperature of the neck of the bottle. For a fraction of a second, the temperature may drop to as low as thirty-one degrees Fahrenheit below zero. It's over so fast that you never realize it. Otherwise, your fingers would be frozen onto the glass bottle.

There is nothing like a nice foamy head on a glass of cold beer. The head is formed by the release of uncounted gas bubbles. Beer bubbles are born from minute clusters of CO_2 molecules that gather on microscopic cracks and pits in the beer mug or tiny bits of floating matter in the beer. When a glass of beer is poured, tiny pockets of air can be trapped on these pits in the glass. The trapped air bubbles attract CO_2 molecules, which grow into bubbles. At these spots on the glass, where large numbers of gas molecules have accumulated, a long string of bubbles can be created that seem to stream upward like a never-ending string of golden pearls. As they rise to the surface, the bubbles attract more gas and grow larger and rise faster (the same process explains the rising of bubbles when you boil water).

When you shake salt into your beer and create that exciting explosion of bubbles, it is not a chemical reaction of salt and beer that's taking place. It's due to the fact that salt grains, on a microscopic level, are very pitted and cracked and offer CO_2 molecules excellent places to accumulate. Any similar grainy substance will produce the same effect, even sand. Most people, however, will not want to dump sand into their beer.

In order to get a nice head on the beer, it must be poured into the glass in such a way as to swirl the beer about. The swirling motion of the beer causes minute changes in pressure within the beer, which causes the gas to expand into bubbles, making the hoped-for head. If your beer head starts to foam over the top of the glass, stick your finger into the foamy head, and it will stop rising. This is because the oils on your skin reduce the surface tension in the beer, causing the bubbles to collapse.

So the next time you have a few at the local pub, spend a few minutes watching that endless line of bubbles spring into life in your glass of ale, while contemplating more weighty matters, such as where you parked your car!

Why do men have Adam's apples?

Actually, both men and women have Adam's apples. In medical terms, the Adam's apple is called a thyroid cartilage. The reason a man's Adam's apple is larger than a woman's is because his larynx is larger to accommodate his longer vocal cords. (By the way, it is men's longer vocal cords that give them deeper voices.) A second reason, which female readers may not enjoy reading, is because women have more fat in their necks, which hides the Adam's apple.

The name, Adam's apple, is taken from the Biblical story of Adam and Eve. As the story goes, a piece of the apple that Eve had given Adam to eat became lodged in his throat. From then on, Adam and all his male descendants had an enlarged larynx as a symbol of Adam's shame.

Why is the National Hockey League Championship Trophy called the Stanley Cup?

The Stanley Cup is the oldest professional sports trophy in North America. The cup was purchased by Canada's then Governor-General, Lord Stanley of Preston, in 1892, for $48.67. The trophy was awarded to the top Canadian amateur hockey teams. In 1910, the National Hockey Association obtained the Stanley Cup as its championship trophy.

The league later became the NHL and the trophy has continued to be its top prize.

Was there ever a real Betty Crocker?

Betty Crocker has been a trusted kitchen friend for over seventy years. Her face has adorned flour and cake mix products for decades and has become associated with quality baking. Betty's familiar persona was, however, created as a public relations aid by a 1920s milling company. A forerunner of General Mills, Inc., the Washburn Crosby Company ran a sales promotion for Gold Medal Flour in 1921. They offered consumers a pincushion shaped like a sack of flour if they could complete a jigsaw puzzle of a flour milling scene. Thousands of entries poured in, many of them with questions concerning baking problems.

A man named Sam Gabe, the company's advertising manager, thought it would be appropriate for a woman to answer the letters. Taking the last name of a recently retired company executive, William G. Crocker, and a friendly sounding first name, Betty, a fictitious name was created to sign the responses to inquiries.

A woman from the company with nice handwriting was chosen to sign "Betty Crocker." Her signature is the one still in use today. In 1924, "Betty Crocker" started doing food service programs on the radio. By 1936, Betty was so popular that a face was needed to go with the created persona. A portrait was commissioned from the prominent New York artist Neysa McMein. In the portrait, McMein blended the facial characteristics of several of the women working in the company's Home Service Department into a motherly image, which was used for nearly twenty years.

Betty has changed over the years. In 1955, she was repainted into a softer, smiling version of the original image. She was modernized again in 1965 and 1968. In 1972, to placate the growing feminist movement, Betty became more businesslike and stiff looking, more like an accountant than someone you would expect to find in the kitchen baking brownies. Her image was softened again in 1980 to picture someone all women could identify with.

While she has changed dramatically over the years, a few things have stayed the same: Betty has always had dark hair, blue eyes, and a red dress. Apparently men don't buy these products, or Betty would have been a buxom blond in a red bikini.

Why do the symbols ♂ and ♀ represent male and female?

No, these are not anatomical representations. Shame on you! They are symbols related to Greek mythology. The female symbol ♀ is supposed to represent a woman holding a hand mirror and is associated with Aphrodite, the Greek goddess of beauty. The male symbol ♂ represents a spear and shield and is associated with the Greek god of war, Ares. The male and female symbols also represent the planets Mars and Venus (the Roman god of war and the Roman goddess of beauty).

Where does the flu come from and why are there different strains every year?

Every summer the Center for Disease Control in Atlanta, Georgia, tries to determine which strains of the influenza virus will be appearing in the United States in the coming winter. By watching worldwide trends, they adjust the influenza vaccine to fight the strains most likely to appear that winter. The vaccine is different every year and protects us from several, but not all, flu viruses. Yearly flu variations are usually minor, involving subtle changes in the viruses' outer coat that don't present a big problem to most people's immune systems.

However, every decade or two, major changes have occurred in the viruses' spiny protein coat, which most human immune systems cannot recognize and fight off, triggering worldwide epidemics. Major outbreaks in the recent past include the Great Pandemic of 1918 (which killed over 21 million people worldwide), the 1957 Asian flu, and the 1968 Hong Kong flu. Why these major flus originate in China and Southeast Asia is being studied.

One theory, presented by two British researchers, zoologist Earnest Naylor and German virologist Christoph Scholtissek, implicate the farming practices common there. In countries like China, they may raise hens, pigs, and fish in one integrated operation. The theory goes that the droppings and leftover food from the pigs feeds the hens. The hen droppings help fertilize the fish ponds.

Sounds like a perfect system, raising three different animals with no waste. All three species, however, may be exchanging viruses among themselves via feces. The birds can pass avian flu viruses to the pigs. In the pigs, the two viruses commingle and form into new varieties that are then passed back to the farmers, whose immune system cannot fight the new virus. It has been proven that the viruses that caused the 1968 Hong Kong flu came from ducks.

Why don't you ever see cashews sold in the shell?

Most nuts, peanuts, walnuts, hazelnuts, almonds, pecans, Brazil nuts, etc., can be bought in the shell. You will never see cashews sold this way, and for a good reason. The oil that surrounds the shell is very irritating to the skin and can cause blisters. (Cashews are in the same plant family as poison ivy.) This makes the harvesting of cashews nasty work. Trying to shell these obnoxious little nuts at home would also be a difficult task. Even roasting the shells causes a noxious smoke to be given off. No one would bother. Hence, the packager does it for you.

Another interesting thing about cashews is that they can help prevent tooth decay. The oil in the nut is so powerful that it inhibits the growth of plaque-producing bacteria. Maybe someday we'll see a new toothpaste on the market. Instead of mint-flavored Crest, we could be brushing with cashew-flavored Crest. Yum!

Who first thought of freezing foods?

If you think it was Clarence Birdseye, think again. The Eskimos have been successfully freezing food, perhaps not by choice, for millenia. However, Clarence Birdseye did perfect the process in warmer climes and introduced it to the world at large. It was already known that cold storage preserved food, but the slow freezing methods tried at the

time took all day, and when thawed for use, the food broke down and became mushy and tasteless.

While working as a fur trader in Labrador in 1912, Birdseye realized that fast freezing of food, as practiced by the Eskimos, was better for preserving foods. He then devised a process of spraying food with a mist of circulating brine at minus forty-five degrees Fahrenheit. He came to learn that quick freezing food inhibited the formation of ice crystals that caused the cell tissues in the food to burst apart. Upon thawing, the cells now remained intact and the food looked and tasted fresh and ready for consumption.

In 1924 Birdseye started a seafood company in Gloucester, Massachusetts. He eventually declared bankruptcy after trying to manufacture and distribute frozen foods. He sold his process and plants in 1929 to a company that later became General Foods Corporation.

What are all those unpronounceable ingredients in shampoos?

Did you ever glance at the list of ingredients in your favorite shampoo while your were showering? It makes for interesting reading and you can try to imagine what all those crazy-sounding chemicals are doing in your shampoo and what they are doing to your hair. The basic cleaning ingredients in shampoos are synthetic detergents, not soap. Detergent rinses cleaner than soap, which reacts with minerals in the water to form a scum.

The most commonly found detergent in shampoo is probably well known to you from your shower-time reading—lauryl sulfate. It has long molecules with one end that attracts water and one end that grabs dirt and grease. When you shampoo, the detergent binds the dirt from your hair to water molecules, which are then rinsed out.

Another ingredient is cocamide DEA, which gives shampoo a nice, rich lather. Lather doesn't do much to help clean hair, but it looks and feels good. Other ingredients that don't do much for cleaning but make the shampoo product more appealing to use are glycol sterate (makes it look pearly or opaque), celluloses (thickening agents), and propylene glycol, a humectant (which helps the hair stay wet).

There are a host of dyes, fragrances, and natural ingredients that are supposed to do everything short of curing baldness. You can find almost any natural additive, such as beer, apricot or any other fruit you can name, herbs, coconut, honey, etc.

One thing you don't want to find is fungi or bacteria. This is why manufacturers add preservatives with those long, unpronounceable methyl-names, such as methylchloroisothiazolinone or methylisothiazolinone. But if some unknown French chemist marketed a new full-body, conditioning, fungal/bacterial formula shampoo for overstressed hair, people would run right out to buy it!

Why does catnip makes cats act "dopey"?

Catnip, or *Nepeta cataria*, is a naturally occurring herb that is the cat world's equivalent of marijuana. Catnip is native to Europe but quickly spread across the United States soon after its introduction by early settlers, who grew it for its medicinal qualities. It is claimed that catnip tea eases intestinal cramps, its juice increases menstrual flow, and that it relieves toothaches when chewed.

Cats, however, don't care about its medicinal uses! They revel in the "high" they get from it. What makes cats act dopey is the oils that are released when the plant tissue is broken. The plants release this oil to prevent insects from eating them. The oil has exactly the opposite effect on cats. They destroy the plant in their effort to release as much of the oil as possible. Apparently the plant didn't evolve this defense mechanism with cats in mind.

While it has been rumored that catnip has mildly hallucinogenic effects on humans, this is not true. However, if you have a cat, you can enjoy its effects vicariously!

What would happen if you never broke a chain letter?

Usually people worry about the opposite scenario—what will happen if they *do* break a chain letter. A typical chain letter details all the dreadful, heinous things that happen to those who receive the letter, and who dare to defy the vile chain letter gods and break the chain. Sometimes also enclosed are actual handwritten endorsements of the letter, signed by several Hollywood celebrities, as if that somehow adds to the mystical quality of the thing!

In a weird kind of way, however, the consequences of not breaking a chain letter can be more disastrous and mind-boggling. The letter's request is usually simple enough—make five copies of the letter and mail it to five friends. Sounds harmless enough, but consider this. If everyone complied with the request, the number of letters and people involved would snowball to enormous numbers in a surprisingly short time. It is what is called the "and they told two friends phenomenon." It would go as follows: You send 5 letters to 5 people, then those 5 people send letters to 25 people, then those 25 send letters to 125 people, they send letters to 625 people, and the progression continues to grow until after just fifteen cycles of the chain process, the number of people receiving the letter reaches an incredible 6,103,515,625!

The volume of letters would quickly exceed the population of the world and, as the process repeats itself, would continue to spiral to astronomical numbers with each successive mailing. Each individual on the planet would be receiving and sending uncounted, never-ending letters, thus crippling the world's postal system and allowing little time to do anything but copy and mail letters, leading to the end of civilization and eventually mankind! No wonder these get-rich-quick schemes are so common and also illegal. So, the next time you get one of these letters, do yourself and your friends a favor, toss it in the garbage. You may suffer some personal misfortune, but it is a small price to pay to save modern civilization.

Why does southern California have such a desirable climate?

Take away the smog, earthquakes, and brush fires and southern California is a great place to live. This is because the area has a Mediterranean-type climate. This type of climate is found only in four other places in the world, the southern tip of Africa, central Chile, southern Australia, and around the Mediterranean Sea. A Mediterranean climate has "warm," wet winters and dry, sunny summers. Low-pressure cells traveling along the West Coast cause the wet winters. High-pressure cells centered off the coast of northern California deflect storms off to the north in the summer and keep things sunny and dry. Along the Pacific coast, upwellings of cold, deep ocean waters keep temperatures mild all summer long. Normal July temperatures are 70° F in San Diego, 74° F in Los Angeles and a cool 62° F in San Francisco. Charleston, South Carolina, which is at roughly the same latitude as San Diego, has a normal July temperature 12 degrees higher, 82° F! So while summer air temperatures may be quite pleasant, the cool ocean waters can be less than inviting.

Why is pink for girls and blue for boys?

In ancient times, the survival of boys was more important than the survival of girls in many cultures. Supposedly, the ancients believed that children had to be protected from evil spirits who preyed upon them. It was felt that blue, the color of the heavens above, could ward off the forces of evil. Therefore, little boys were dressed blue. Why they didn't simply dress all children in blue and thus protect the girls also is a little strange. Perhaps girls were left unprotected as an offering to placate the spirits.

Later in history girls were honored with their very own color, pink, which apparently had no special powers.

Today psychologists are aware of the effects that different colors have on children. It has been shown that pink (not just any pink, but bubble-gum pink) has a soothing effect on children. The color pink is used in many hospital psychiatric wards to calm patients. Curiously enough, the color blue also has a soothing effect. It has been shown to lower a child's blood pressure and increase attentiveness. Could this be another reason for dressing children in pink or blue? Maybe.

Just in case you are curious, yellow cheers and excites children. Red is the worst color for kids to deal with, because it raises blood pressure, respiration and heart rate, and brain and muscle activity. You might want to keep this in mind the next time you paint your child's room!

What exactly is the "Aryan" race?

When we think of the Aryan race, we typically think of blond-haired, blue-eyed Germanic-type people, the race of people that the Nazis thought were superior to the rest of the world. Actually, the word "Aryan" is not a racial term but a language-related term. Far from being from one race, Aryans consisted of a great many peoples who shared an early Indo-European language. True Aryans were really Asiatic invaders who settled in the Indian subcontinent and Persia. Their language spread from there to Europe. The word Aryan is from the Sanskrit, "Arya," meaning "noble." Today, Buddhist Aryans make up a majority of the population of Sri Lanka.

Why are barns painted red?

Some people believe barns are painted red so the cows can find their way home! This is erroneous, as cows don't see colors all that well. (By the way, it is also a fallacy that bulls are excited by the red color of the toreador's cape. It is the motion of the cape and the toreador's taunting of the bull that makes the bull so hostile toward the cape.)

In the early days of barn building, paint, if available, was very expensive and generally was white (i.e., whitewash). The self-reliant farmers, therefore, created their own paint from the richness of the land. The greatest supply of naturally occurring pigment was found in the soil. Many soils contain high levels of iron oxide, which has a redness to it and can be suspended in a solution and used as a coating. It is therefore due to the farmer's thriftiness and ingenuity that barns are red, not because they thought it attractive to Bossy the Cow.

What makes "stainless" steel stainless?

Stainless steel was developed in 1913 by British metallurgist Harry Brearley, who was searching for a better lining for cannons. He discovered that chromium had the ability to create an oxide lining, and that steel made from iron and chromium resisted many corrosive chemicals.

Stainless steel is coated with a thin, transparent film of iron oxide and chromium. This prevents soap, food, water, and air from getting to the metal below and eating it away. Since its coating is so smooth, stainless steel is very sanitary. Bacteria, fungi, and dirt have nowhere to hide and are easily washed away. For this reason, commercial kitchen surfaces and cooking equipment are often made of stainless steel.

Another unique thing about this kind of steel is that it can "heal" itself. When scratched or nicked, the protective oxide immediately recoats the damaged area. Because of its great ability to resist rusting, it is an ideal material for cutlery, pots, and pans.

Now, if they could only make stainless steel mufflers...

Why do we eat the foods we do?

Of the five-hundred-thousand known plants species, man has only domesticated about one hundred. Only about thirty of these species provide us with 85 percent of our food and 95 percent of our protein and calories. Seventy-five percent of all of man's food comes from only eight cereal species—corn, rice, wheat, oats, barley, sorghum, millet, and rye. Of the forty-five hundred mammal species on Earth, only sixteen have been domesticated for man's use.

Why is it that we are content to subsist on the relatively few plant and animal species that ancient man chose to domesticate thousands of years ago? Surely there are other species that we could cultivate or breed for new food sources. As a matter of fact, there is now a worldwide search being conducted to find new species for food. Particular attention is being paid to find species that are nutritious and tasty, and can be raised on land that is currently unsuitable for crops or livestock, such as deserts and swampy areas. Five American plant species that have potential as future food crops are listed below:

1. Buffalo Gourd *(Cucurbita foetidissima)*, a desert melon, has two sources of food. The plant's huge root can reach two hundred pounds and is loaded with starch. The melon's seeds are rich in protein and polyunsaturated oil.
2. Groundnut *(Apios americana)* is a sweet, starchy tuber that the Pilgrims survived on during their first few winters. It was a popular staple of East Coast Indians. Groundnut supposedly has eight times the protein of potatoes.

3. Hog peanut *(Amphicarpa bracteata)* has large edible seeds high in protein and rich in oil.
4. Tepary bean *(Phaseolus acutifolius)* is found along the Mexican border and can withstand very arid conditions. The Indians of New Mexico and Arizona cultivate it.
5. Prairie potato *(Psoralea esculenta)* was grown by the Plains Indian. It has a protein content three times that of the conventional potato.

The "farming" of unusual animals as food sources is also being explored. The wide assortment of creatures being raised for food include: frogs, toads, snails, butterflies, water buffalo, crawfish, crocodiles, turtles, deer, antelope, and several others. We could someday be enjoying dinners of grilled water buffalo, prairie potatoes, and desert melons.

Why does the bridge freeze before the road surface does?

In many northern states there are road signs before every interstate highway overpass warning drivers that the "Bridge Freezes Before Road Surface." The main difference between a road surface on a bridge and on the ground is that a bridge is surrounded by air, whereas the road has earth beneath it. The earth acts as a heat sink, which changes in temperature much more slowly than the air.

Therefore, if there is a drop in air temperature, a wet bridge surface will be surrounded by cold air. The road surface will have cold air above, but will be insulated from the cold from below by the earth and thus will not freeze as suddenly as the bridge surface.

Was Nipper, the RCA mascot, a real dog?

Yes, Nipper, the fox terrier, was originally portrayed in a painting titled *His Master's Voice* by artist Francis Barraud.

He took over the care of Nipper after his brother, the dog's owner, died. Barraud was amazed at Nipper's fascination in listening to a recording of his brother's voice on his gramophone and captured this scene on canvas.

The original painting included his brother's casket, which Barraud painted out upon selling this work to the Gramophone Company, Ltd.

"Nipper" later became the property of the Victor Talking Machine Company and then of RCA, in 1928.

What is the origin of the "wave" at large sporting events?

This phenomenon of adjoining sections of spectators standing up, raising their arms, and sitting back down in sequence, thus creating a wavelike appearance, is of recent origin. It suddenly appeared during a game one day in 1981 and caught on like wildfire. The man with the best claim to "inventing" it is George Henderson, aka "Krazy George." Krazy George is a professional cheerleader. He can be seen occasionally at NFL games in Houston and Minnesota banging his little drum and generally harassing the opposing teams. On October 15, 1981, he was working a playoff game between the Yankees and the Oakland A's in Oakland Coliseum. Midway through the game, he had a now famous inspiration. He went from section to section of the crowd asking them to stand up, yell, and sit down. The first time only the first few sections complied, then seven more, and by the third attempt the wave went right around the stadium and continued.

Apparently, another man named Bill Bissell also claims to have created the wave independently at the University of Washington a scant two weeks after the nationally televised Oakland Coliseum game, as coincidental as that may sound. His version of the story is that at a 1981 Husky's football game, a former Washington cheerleader, Robb Weller (yes, the Robb Weller who cohosted the TV show "Entertainment Tonight" at the time), led a cheer where members of different sororities and fraternities would stand up and sit down in sequence. It caught on and kept going. The origin of the wave may be open for debate, but people at games seem to love it, and it has quickly spread across the country and around the world.

Why is a "Baltimore chop" in baseball called by that name?

A Baltimore chop is a batted ball that hits the ground at home plate, or close to the plate, and then bounces high in the air, allowing the batter to reach first base safely before a play can be made. This hitting tactic was perfected in the 1890s by Wee Willie Keeler of the old Baltimore Orioles, hence the name, Baltimore chop.

Why was lead added to gasoline in the first place?

Cars in the early 1920s had a problem of cylinder knocking which thwarted the development of more fuel-efficient engines. Engine knocking, known as preignition, is caused by premature spontaneous ignition of the hydrocarbons in a gasoline, due to the high temperatures and pressure inside an engine cylinder, thus resulting in the characteristic "knock." The director of General Motors Research Corporation, Charles F. Kettering (later of Sloan-Kettering Institute for Cancer Research fame), spent several years, and $25 million, working on this problem. He discovered that adding tetraethyl lead to gasoline increased an engine's performance and efficiency.

He found that adding tetraethyl lead to gas improved its octane rating, which is a measure of a fuel's ability to resist preignition. Octane ratings are obtained by comparing a gas with a mixture of octane and heptane. A gasoline with an antiknock performance equal to a mixture of 90 percent octane and 10 percent heptane has an octane rating of 90.

In 1924, General Motors and Standard Oil started manufacturing the additive and it was used continuously in the United States until 1985, when the Environmental Protection Agency mandated its gradual phaseout.

Some of you may remember the sales gimmick where Gulf Oil gave out two plastic horseshoes to stick on the back of your car, symbolizing the "kick" their leaded gas gave your engine. Your car's engine, however, kicked a great deal of lead into the air around urban areas. The EPA also mandated cleaner burning engines, equipped with catalytic converters, which remove other harmful pollutants from a car's exhaust.

The newer, cleaner burning gasoline contains more oxygen and far less other octane-increasing additives. The price for cleaner air wasn't cheap, as refiners had to retool and more efficient car engines had to be developed. Of course, all these expenses are ultimately passed along to the consumer, but it's a small price to pay for cleaner air.

Why are certain "American" English words spelled differently in "British" English?

Before the late eighteenth century, English writers generally believed that as long as the reader could understand what was being written, the spelling of words did not matter. Another problem with establishing a uniform English spelling was that the alphabet was borrowed from another language, Roman. The Roman alphabet was never intended to represent English sounds. It was adopted from the Greek alphabet and had only 20 letters, lacking J, K, V, W, Y, and Z. The Romans added K (for abbreviations) and Y and Z (for words they took from the Greek). These twenty-three letters became the early English alphabet. Later, W was added by joining together (you guessed it) two U's. J and V were introduced in the post-Shakespearean era, about 1630, to represent the consonant sounds of I and U. Later in the eighteenth century, elementary dictionaries began to appear in England, promoting the idea of uniform spelling.

An Englishman living in the American Colonies, Noah Webster, hoped that establishing a proper American spelling of the English language would give America the true mark of culture.

Noah Webster was born in Hartford, Connecticut, in 1758. A lawyer turned teacher, he wrote textbooks during the Revolutionary War. He won fame in 1783 by publishing his book "The Blue-Backed" *American Speller,* which, helped by American cultural insecurity, went on to sell a whopping 80 million copies and was second only to the Bible in sales. He earned a royalty of one cent per copy, which afforded him a very good standard of living and allowed him to pursue other linguistic endeavors.

His goal was not only the standardization of English in America but the separation of American English from British English. According to Webster, "Our honor requires us to have a system of our own, in language as well as government." Noah felt he was improving the English language. He went from printer to printer imploring them to spell words his way (e.g., theater, not theatre). He set about writing the *American Dictionary of the English Language,* which was published in 1828. We can credit Webster for the spelling of the following English words: center for centre, color for colour, fiber for fibre, defense for defence, tire for tyre, as well as numerous others. For all its impact and later popularity, Webster's first dictionary sold a mere 2,500 copies and he died, in debt, in 1843.

The remarkable uniformity of spoken American English can also be partially credited to Webster. He preached the proper enunciation of each syllable in each word. For example, Americans should say "sec-re-tary," not se-cret'ry," as the British do. He also pushed for the homogeneity of American English, as opposed to the many regional peculiarities of British English.

Webster might be horrified if he heard the differences in dialect today between the Deep South and New England. However, he would undoubtedly be pleased at the way American English, spread through music, films, books, and the media, is being adopted around the world.

What are graham crackers made of?

The obvious answer would be graham, but what is graham? This is an easy one. Graham crackers are made of graham flour; graham flour is simply whole wheat flour. It was promoted by a nineteenth-century Presbyterian minister named Sylvester Graham. He was very active in the temperance movement. Graham felt that eating a healthful diet could cure alcoholism, aid digestion, and lead to a more wholesome lifestyle. His keen interest in bowel regularity led the press to nickname him "the peristaltic persuader."

Graham traveled through the United States preaching the evils of eating meats and fats, which he was sure led to sexual promiscuity. His answer to man's lack of virtue was a diet of vegetables, fruits, and unsifted whole wheat flour in place of white bread. His many followers helped make the use of "graham" flour popular and his legacy lives on today in the form of graham crackers. So if you ever feel the need to cleanse your soul, get a box of graham crackers and a glass of milk, and think pious thoughts.

Why do cows lie down before it rains?

Cows aren't the smartest creatures around. They couldn't care less if it were raining, snowing, or sunny. They don't plan whether to lie down according to the weather. Some-

times they will stand in the rain or lie down in the mud. Such is a cow's life. They lie down any time.

Cows are docile, lazy animals. As ruminants, they must eat a lot of food, and they also have very slow digestive systems. Cows evolved as animals of who were preyed upon, and lying down was a good way to hide from the predators. Occasional lying down during the day affords them some leisurely digestion time out of the sight of predators. Their famous weather-predicting skills are purely an old wives' tale.

Why aren't there any skyscrapers in the middle of the Manhattan skyline but several at either end?

The skyline of Manhattan is one of the world's most famous and beautiful. One distinctive feature of the panoramic New York City skyline is the absence of tall buildings in the middle. There is a big gap in the skyline between the Empire State Building in midtown and the World Trade Center to the south. This building arrangement is not accidental and has to do with the geology of Manhattan Island.

Skyscrapers are very heavy structures and require solid foundations. The midtown and downtown areas of Manhattan sit on bedrock close to the surface. The area of the building gap lies on much softer ground, where the bedrock lies deeper. The cost of driving piles is prohibitive.

In Los Angeles, high-rise buildings were not allowed to be built, prior to 1957, because of the ever-present threat of earthquakes. With the development of earthquake-stress technology and improved building designs, taller structures were allowed.

Skyscrapers were first designed and built in the United States. They evolved from the desire of American businessmen to be able to operate in close proximity to one another. For this reason, skyscrapers tend to be clumped together in urban business centers, as they are on the lower tip of Manhattan. Seldom do they stand alone.

The development of higher and higher buildings paralleled the advances that were made in structural supports and elevators. The replacement of masonry walls with metal I-beams enabled skyscrapers to soar. However, tall buildings require a fast mode of up and down transportation. What good is a tall building if you have to walk up hundreds of stairs? By 1880, elevators were adequate for ten-story buildings; by 1890, they could reach up to twenty stories. The higher the elevators could reach, the higher the building could go.

The increasing height of skyscrapers created problems of traffic congestion, difficulties in firefighting, and increased water demand. Property values around skyscrapers also climbed dramatically. Regulation of their construction was clearly needed and was provided by the New York Zoning Ordinance of 1916. It limited the height of a building in proportion to the breadth of the street it faced. If a building were to exceed this designated height, its upper floors had to lie behind a diagonal line drawn from the center of the street and passing through the designated height. Thus the stepped-back design of the upper floors of many tall buildings inside and outside of New York.

Another problem of having tall buildings clumped together, such as in the Wall Street area, is the lack of adequate light and air circulation to reach the occupants of the lower levels. To avoid this problem, architects began to design building complexes with taller structures separated by lower buildings. This is the case with New York's Rockefeller Center.

Why is the area of a ballpark where the pitchers warm up called a bullpen?

No one is entirely sure how this term came to be. The most probable explanation is that, in the old days, pitchers used to loosen their throwing arms along the sides of the playing field, between the foul lines and fences. The Bull Durham Tobacco Company was a big baseball advertiser at that time. Their signs, which sported a huge bull staring down at the field, were placed on the fences of ballparks in 1909. In many ballparks the pitchers warmed up directly in front of these giant bulls. Hence, that area of the field became known as the bull pen.

Another possible explanation is that in the late 1800s spectators stood in confined, roped-off areas near the outfield fence, called bull pens. As grandstands were eventually built in more and more ballparks, this area was no longer needed for spectators. Some ballparks utilize this area for pitcher warm-ups.

Why do Wint-O-Green Life Savers spark when you bite into them?

Next time you need a thrill on a dull evening, grab your loved one and some Wint-O-Green Life Savers and head for the bathroom. Turn out the light and face the mirror. Tightly clench the Life Saver between your teeth with your lips apart while biting down hard enough to crack the candy. You should see a flash of eerie blue-green light. Fascinating yes, but easily explainable.

When sugar crystal molecules are ripped apart, opposite electric charges are created on either side of the break, causing electrons to leap across the crack in the candy. These electrons excite the nitrogen in the air, causing it to emit the blue-green flashes akin to lightning.

What makes Wint-O-Green candy different than other hard sugar candies is the wintergreen it contains. Wintergreen contains fluorescent methyl salicylate, which absorbs ultraviolet light and converts it into light that we can see. Unfortunately, while Wintergreen Life Savers' taste is reliable, their sparking ability is not. Any background light can hamper the effect, as can humidity in the air. A similar sparking phenomenon can be produced by certain cellophane tape adhesives when pulled away from a surface in the dark.

Now that you have gotten your loved one into the darkened room, impressed him or her with your knowledge, and have fresh wintergreen breath, the rest is up to you!

What is ozone?

Ozone is simply another form of oxygen. We are all familiar with O_2 (two oxygen atoms bound together), which we breathe. Ozone is O_3, a molecule of three oxygen atoms.

Ozone may have played a key role in forming the O_2 we all take for granted. The early Earth contained many nasty gases and water (H_2O), but not much oxygen. Ozone breaks down H_2O into its component parts—hydrogen and oxygen. The hydrogen, being very light, would have been blown off into space, leaving behind the O_2, thus enabling the creation of life.

Today, the ozone forms a vital layer of the atmosphere in the upper stratosphere that reflects the dangerous wavelengths of ultraviolet (UV) light back into space. Ultraviolet light of slightly longer wavelengths can pass through the atmosphere and enable some careful sunbathers to acquire their beautiful tans and imprudent sunbathers to burn.

The problem we face today is the depletion of the ozone layer by modern technology and the increased risks of skin cancer. Skin cancer will afflict six hundred thousand Americans this year alone, and eventually one out of seven of us. So much for sunbathing! One cause for concern is modern jetliners, such as the supersonic transports (SSTs). These planes fly higher than most, into the stratosphere, and their exhaust contains nitrous oxides which can find their way into the nearby ozone layer and destroy ozone. This is one reason that the United States doesn't have a fleet of SSTs.

The other major problem is the use of propellants for aerosols and refrigerants, such as freon, that contain chlorofluorocarbons, (CF_2Cl_2 and $CFCl_3$). Chlorofluorocarbons, when released into the atmosphere, break down into chlorine atoms which destroy ozone. Chlorine acts as a catalyst in the chemical breakdown of ozone. Since the lifetime of a chlorine atom in the stratosphere is from five to ten years, it can continue to destroy ozone for a long time. For this reason the United States imposed a ban on all nonessential use of fluorocarbons in 1977.

Ozone is naturally created in the stratosphere and also naturally destroyed by UV light. The amount of stratospheric ozone varies with the eleven-year solar cycle of sunspot activity. Unexpected holes in the ozone layer have recently been found over the polar regions where the ozone layer is supposed to be at its thickest. A hole the size of the United States that appears every autumn has been found over Antarctica. Whether or not this is a naturally occurring phenomenon remains to be seen.

Generally speaking, the closer you move toward the equator, the thinner the ozone layer becomes. So it is much easier to sunburn in southern Florida than in Maine, and the risks of getting skin cancer are that much greater.

Why is the moon covered with craters but not the earth?

The moon and the Earth are billions of years old, but, astronomically speaking, they are only a stone's throw away from each other. How can it be then, that the moon today is covered with craters, while the Earth has very few large craters?

Most craters on the moon are believed to have been formed by meteorite impacts some 4 billion years ago. During the next billion or so years, volcanoes on the moon spewed forth lava, filling in large areas of these craters.

Similar events were happening on the Earth up to this point in history. About 3 billion years ago, the moon became geologically inactive and the meteoritic bombardment ceased. The Earth, however, has continued to change geologically. Volcanoes continue to spew forth; the continents continue to move; etc. The forces of water and wind erosion have scoured the Earth clean of all but the most recent craters.

It is believed by some that a massive comet or asteroid smashed into the Earth some 65 million years ago and is responsible for the extinction of the dinosaurs. It is very likely that the impact occurred in the Gulf of Mexico or the Caribbean Sea. A crater, discovered on the Yucatan Peninsula and long covered over by sediment, may be where the object hit. It threw up a cloud of debris that filled the atmosphere, blocking out sunlight and reducing Earth's temperature. The cold-blooded dinosaurs were doomed.

Another large crater was recently discovered off the coast of Nova Scotia, Canada. It is thirty miles in diameter and is thought to have been caused about 50 million years ago by an object one mile in diameter.

The best example of an impact crater in the United States is Meteor Crater near Winslow, Arizona. The meteorite weighed about 270,000 tons and made a hole about 575 feet deep and three-quarters of a mile wide. It landed twenty thousand years ago, only a blink of an eye in geological time, so you never know...

Why are short naps called catnaps?

As anyone who has owned a cat knows, they don't lead a very strenuous life. In fact, cats sleep away about 80 percent of their lives. Cats and human beings obviously don't have the same sleep patterns. Our sleep cycle has several stages that take us in and out of sleep. Cats, however, just drop off into sleep. They don't get drowsy first and drift into slumber. Instead of going into a long, deep sleep, they have rather short sleep cycles. They will wake up periodically, look around or listen to make sure all is safe and then fall back to sleep again. This sequence can occur several times in a row, hence the term "cat nap."

Why is the core of the earth so hot?

The core of the earth is made up primarily of iron and nickel. Outside the core is another layer called the mantle, and above that is the thin layer we live on, the crust. The very center of the core is probably solid and the outer part is probably a very dense liquid. The source of heat at the earth's center results from the tremendous pressure of compression and natural radioactivity.

Because certain forms of isotopes (chemical elements with differing numbers of neutrons) are unstable, they spontaneously undergo nuclear reactions. These reactions produce high-energy particles, such as electrons and helium nuclei, that collide with the atoms in the rock of the earth's interior and produce heat. There is enough radioactive material in the earth to cause intense heat. The mantle layer surrounding the core is a poor conductor of heat, helping to insulate the core and trap the heat within.

When the earth formed from a mass of space debris, it coalesced into a sphere. The great heat created by the earth's compression caused the iron to melt and sink to the center, forming the core. As the earth eventually cooled over billions of years, various materials, due to their differing densities and freezing points, hardened at different distances from the core, thus forming the stratified layers of the earth that exist today.

The temperature at the center of the earth is thought to be around thirteen thousand degrees Fahrenheit, hotter than the surface of the sun. Much of the earth's original radioactive material ended up in the upper layers of the earth. Therefore, heat is also produced not far below the ground. This upper heat layer lies between the crust and the mantle. The heat in this layer is not hot enough to melt the rock but does make it soft and plastic. On this soft layer plates of the crust float and cause the continental drift. Areas where two plates are moving away from each other, called rifts, tend to be geologically active, with molten material being pushed to the surface through vents such as volcanoes and geysers.

Places where two plates rub against each other are prone to earthquake activity. Mountains can be formed in areas where plates push into one another.

What's the difference between a rutabaga and a turnip?

If you're like most people, you never knew what grandma served at Thanksgiving, rutabagas or turnips. The names seem to be used synonymously. Dear granny may have been a good cook, but she was no botanist.

The rutabaga (Winter or Swedish turnip) and the common turnip are often both called by the common name, turnip. However, they are entirely different plants. Rutabagas *(Brassica napobrassica)* are similar to turnips botanically but do not resemble them in appearance. They have smooth, shiny blue-green foliage, a large tuber, a long leafy neck, and a firmer flesh than a turnip. By contrast, the common turnip *(Brassica rapa)*, has hairy leaves and the tuber is white-fleshed, smaller and flatter than the rutabaga.

Store-bought rutabagas have been waxed in hot paraffin diluted with beeswax, resin, or mineral oil to reduce shrinkage during shipping and marketing. They don't really grow into that large, waxy, candlelike vegetable you find in the produce section.

How do African women balance and carry such heavy loads on their heads?

Balance and posture are the keys to this technique, which young East African girls learn from their mothers. They begin by walking around balancing very small, light objects, much like an American girl balancing a book on her head to develop grace. By the time they are young women, they can carry up to 25 percent of their body weight without using

any more energy than they would wearing a straw hat. The reason they can do this is their remarkable posture control. They form a rigid straight line between their vertebrae and pelvis. When they walk there is very little movement of the head, neck, or shoulders. The hips bob somewhat but the ankles and knees do most of the moving.

By bobbing and dipping, we Westerners waste a lot of energy when we walk. African women very efficiently put their energy into forward movement with little needless motion. While African women can carry up to seventy-five pounds on their heads for great distances, most men of the world would be winded in short order carrying that weight in a backpack. These women, in fact, can carry greater weights relative to body size more efficiently than pack mules!

What is a whirling dervish?

The whirling dervish was the name of a Muslim order founded in the thirteenth century by the Persian poet Jalal al-Din al-Rumi, or Mawlana. His name alone is enough to make your head spin. Mawlana was a Persian poet and a mystic. An Islamic fraternity grew up around him. Members of this fraternity gained the nickname of "whirling dervishes" because of the hypnotic gyrating dance they performed as part of their religious rituals. While the dance looks helter-skelter, each movement is specially choreographed and the dance is supposed to lead to ecstasy and higher truth, if not a total loss of equilibrium.

What poisonous plants do we grow in our garden and eat every day?

Some of our garden fruit and vegetable plants are poisonous to varying degrees. We don't necessarily eat the poisonous parts of these plants but it is interesting to note what they are.

Apricot pits, for example, can be fatal if ingested. The pit contains cyanogenetic glycosides, which are converted into cyanide upon digestion. Some hours after ingestion the following symptoms may develop: abdominal pain, vomiting, lethargy, and sweating. In severe cases the victim may become comatose or develop tetanic convulsions.

Potatoes belong to the deadly nightshade family. The toxic parts of a potato are the uncooked sprout and the sun-green skin. There is little toxicity for adults, but some fatalities have been reported in young children.

The stems and leaves of tomato plants are covered with stinging hair, which consists of long, needlelike spines that break off when touched and inject poisons (histamines and acetylcholine) into the skin. This can produce a stinging or burning sensation.

Rhubarb, which is commonly grown for its edible leaf stalks, has leaves that are toxic when eaten in large quantities. They are very corrosive to the stomach lining.

Everyone's favorite poisonous plant, tobacco, is a well documented chronic (long-term) toxin when smoked or chewed. When eaten, as in a salad, tobacco leaves are immediately toxic. Ingestion of nicotine can cause salivation, nausea, sweating, and convulsions. Failure of the muscles that control breathing (a curarelike action) can suddenly appear. So the next time you tell someone to quit smoking tobacco, just be glad they are not eating it!

The following list outlines some other common household plants and their adverse affects:

Azalea and Rhododendron—all plant parts are poisonous; causes paralysis of limbs, abdominal problems, convulsions, watering of nose and eyes.

Daffodil—bulbs poisonous; causes abdominal problems (vomiting, diarrhea, nausea, etc.).

Diffenbachia—all parts poisonous; causes lip and tongue swelling.

English Ivy—all parts poisonous; causes severe abdominal problems.

Holly—berries poisonous; causes abdominal problems (vomiting, diarrhea, nausea, etc.).

Hyacinth—bulbs, leaves and flowers poisonous; causes abdominal problems.

Hydrangea—leaves and buds poisonous; causes abdominal problems, weakness, dizziness, stupor, and convulsions.

Iris—rhizome (bulb) poisonous; causes abdominal problems.

Morning Glory—seeds poisonous (related to LSD); causes hallucinations, abdominal problems, slowed reflexes.

Oleander—tiny leaves deadly; can stop an adult's heart.

Pear—seeds, leaves, bark, and stem poisonous; causes abdominal problems, weakness, respiratory trouble, stupor, convulsions.

Philodendron—all parts poisonous; causes lips and tongue to swell.

Sweet Pea—pea or seed poisonous; causes weak pulse and respiratory trouble, convulsions.

Yew—seeds and leaves poisonous; causes gastroenteritis and cardiac disturbances (however, the red berry *around* the seed is harmless and quite sweet and tasty, but *do not swallow the seed in the berry*).

What gives gin its distinctive flavor?

A gin and tonic, or "G&T" as Londoners call it, is probably the most popular cocktail in England. However, during Victorian times the upper class looked down upon gin and felt it to be fit only for the lower classes.

London gin is made from a base of neutral spirits of grain alcohol which is flavored with juniper berries and coriander. Other natural flavorings that can be added to obtain a desired flavor include angelica root, calamus, cardamom, cassia, lemon peel, orange peel, and orris root. (Sloe gin is a sweet cordial made from the sloeberry, and it is not related to London gin.)

It is the common juniper berry which gives gin its distinctive flavor and aroma.

Just squeeze a juniper berry sometime. If you close your eyes and take a good whiff, you will swear you are actually sniffing a bottle of gin.

How does yeast make bread rise?

Yeasts are one-celled fungal organisms. One ounce of yeast contains 200 billion cells. Yeast has unique properties that mankind has been exploiting since before 4000 B.C. The ancient Egyptians used yeast to make beer, wine, and bread. The Egyptians were the first to make leavened bread.

The production of both alcoholic beverages and leavened bread utilizes yeasts, such as *Saccharomyces cerevisiae*.

Yeasts break down or ferment sugar into alcohol and carbon dioxide (CO_2). Bakers take advantage of yeast's production of CO_2 to make bread light and airy. Baker's yeast is grown in huge vats of molasses and other nutrients. It is then dried and packaged with starch for home use.

When making dough, yeast is mixed with flour, water, and salt. The proteins in wheat flour form gluten, a tenacious elastic substance that gives the dough its cohesiveness during kneading. When the dough is kneaded, the proteins in the flour arrange themselves so that they can trap the CO_2 produced by the yeast as it ferments the sugars in the flour. The trapped CO_2 creates a large number of pores in the bread that make it rise. As the dough rises, the yeast cells become separated from the nutrients and the process gradually slows down. Kneading the dough again will renew the process, causing it to rise again.

Where does the alcohol go that is produced by the fermentation? Actually the alcohol content of the dough just before baking can be as high as 0.5 percent, about one-sixth as much as is found in beer. Most of this alcohol is released as the bread is baked.

Why do we call toll roads "turnpikes"?

We all hate getting stuck at toll plaza backups on the country's many pay roads. Not only do we lose travel time and sometimes our tempers, but we have to *pay* for the privilege. In today's world of big government and taxes on virtually everything, including gasoline, you would think there would be no toll roads or turnpikes. The problem, however, is not a recent development.

The first pay road was a Persian military road built around 2000 B.C., which ran between Syria and Babylon. The first American toll road was built in Virginia in 1785. Another toll road, built in 1795 and surfaced with stone, covered the sixty-three miles between Philadelphia and Lancaster, Pennsylvania. By 1810, 175 private toll-road companies operated some three thousand miles of roadway in New England.

During the early 1800s the federal government was much smaller and stingier than it is today. By 1817, only one major highway, the National Road, had been built. It eventually stretched from Cumberland, Maryland, to Vandalia, Illinois. President James Madison frowned on the use of federal monies for road construction. For this reason several thousand miles of state-chartered private toll roads and bridges were built and maintained through monies collected. These toll roads were called "turnpikes" because they were barricaded every so many miles by turnstiles or piked poles that prevented the traveler from passing through without paying a fee. The piked poles had to be turned to allow the person to pass. Hence the name turnpike.

The word turnpike is said to have first been used in England in 1663. By 1825, most turnpike companies were losing money due to the high costs of road maintenance, and state and local governments took over the building and maintenance of roads.

Early roads were quite crude by today's standards, as were early vehicles. Most roads were not surfaced and travel was a bumpy, dusty ordeal. Those that were surfaced were macadamized (covered with crushed stone). Roads that went through swampy areas were covered with logs laid side by side. The log roads were called "corduroy" roads, which in turn became the name of the welted fabric used in clothing today.

During the Depression of the thirties, there was a renewed interest in toll roads. They became popular after World War II because there was not enough tax money to build the new roads that the burgeoning country needed.

That answers the question of why we call toll roads turnpikes. Perhaps a better question is why we still have these archaic road systems, which literally make you throw your money out the window. Hats off to Connecticut for ripping down the toll booths on its turnpike and restoring free travel to the state. By the same "token," California, home of the "freeway," should be booed for considering the installation of toll booths on some of its highways.

Why are the Rockies higher and more jagged than the Appalachians?

It is simply a matter of age. The Rockies are relatively young as mountains go. They were created approximately 65 million years ago by the uplifting of the Earth's crust, which formed these jagged rocky outcroppings.

The Appalachians formed in much the same way over 300 million years ago. At that time the Appalachians probably resembled the Rockies in shape and size. However, mountains, like people, deteriorate over time. Wind and water erosion wear the mountains down, reducing their height and rounding their edges. Eventually, the Appalachians will become hills and then plains as time marches on.

Why do pigs like rolling around in the mud?

Down through the ages, pigs have picked up the bad reputation of being dirty animals. Far from being filthy creatures, pigs are quite clean if given sanitary living conditions.

The ancient Egyptians held the pig to be sacred and thus ritual cleansing was necessary for people in contact with them. From this stemmed the belief that swine are unclean animals and the Jewish and Muslims came to forbid eating the flesh of pigs. Another reason swine are considered dirty may be for their practice of rolling around in mud.

While it may look like a disgusting habit that pigs engage in for sheer pleasure, there is actually a biological necessity for this behavior. Pigs have no sweat glands and cannot get rid of excess heat by perspiring as we humans do. One good way for pigs to cool off is to moisten their skin and allow the process of evaporation to carry heat away. Some of the energy (heat) used in evaporation comes from the skin.

Since pigs usually aren't kept near pools of clean water, they make do with whatever moisture is handy—namely, mud. This is not to say that they don't thoroughly enjoy themselves in the process.

Why does shower steam set off the smoke alarm?

You just get the baby to sleep and tiptoe into the bathroom for a nice, hot shower before bed. As you emerge from the shower, warm and relaxed, you open the bathroom door and a cloud of steam escapes and triggers the smoke alarm. Not only is the alarm ringing but the baby is screaming and you have to run wet and naked down to the circuit breaker to turn off the alarm. So much for your peaceful evening. Don't blame the smoke alarm, it's just doing its job.

Smoke alarms detect particulate matter in the air. Smoke is made up of airborne particles of burned material. Steam is made up of particles (droplets) of water.

There are two types of smoke alarms. Ionization alarms detect atomic particles, and photoelectric alarms "see" particles. Particles of steam can trick both types and trigger the alarm. While smoke detectors aren't fussy as to the type of particles they detect, just remember that it's better to be safe than sorry. So don't forget to reset the circuit breaker after the steam clears.

Why is Missouri called the "Show-Me State"?

Missouri has been proudly called the "Show-Me State" for almost one hundred years, but no one seems to know what they are so proud about! Even the Missouri secretary of state has no explanation for the state motto.

Supposedly, in the 1890s, the saying was used in poems and songs; no one knows where it originated. The person responsible for popularizing the expression was Missouri congressman Willard D. Vandiver. In 1899, during a speech, Vandiver stated, "I'm from Missouri, you've got to show me." The saying is supposed to imply that Missourians are "tough-minded demanders of proof," although they have no proof that this is what "show me" originally meant.

As for the name Missouri, there is little doubt that it derived from the Sioux tribe of the Indian state called Missouris, the Indian word meaning "town of large canoes."

The following states also have interesting nicknames: Connecticut—the "Nutmeg State." No they don't grow nutmeg in Connecticut. The nickname refers to Yankee ingenuity. Connecticut Yankees were said to be clever enough to make and sell wooden nutmegs in place of the genuine articles.

Oklahoma—the "Sooner State." In 1830, Oklahoma was

known as the Indian Territory. Indians east of the Mississippi River were to be resettled farther west, and several tribes were placed in Oklahoma. In 1889, white homesteaders began to settle there.

At noon on April 22, 1889, the homesteaders were allowed to race across the border in to Oklahoma Territory and stake their land claim. Apparently, many homesteaders jumped the gun and entered Oklahoma too soon. These anxious settlers, who were the first into the new territory, were dubbed "sooners."

Tennessee—the "Volunteer State." During the Mexican War, in 1847, Tennessee governor Aaron Vail Brown issued a call for 2,800 volunteer soldiers. To his surprise, a whopping 30,000 Tennessee patriots turned out to volunteer.

Wisconsin—the "Badger State." Many of the state's early settlers worked in the local lead mines and dug their homes into the sides of the surrounding hills, much like badgers.

Minnesota—"Land of 10,000 Lakes." Minnesota actually has 14,215 lakes.

Why are there ten pins in bowling?

The origins of bowling are at least seven thousand years old. We know that the Egyptians played a game like bowling and even the cavemen may have played a somewhat similar game.

The ancient Polynesians also played a game using a type of alley in which the players stood sixty feet away and tried to knock down a target. Coincidentally, this is exactly the same length as today's bowling alley. In twelfth-century England, round boulders were rolled down cinder or clay alleys at wooden pins.

The fourteenth-century Germans were said to have enjoyed a bowlinglike game, in which a bottle-shaped club, called a kegel, was the target. The players would place a kegel at one end of a cloister of a church and try to knock it down with a stone thrown from the other end. Successfully tipping over the kegel was supposed to be a sign of having lived a

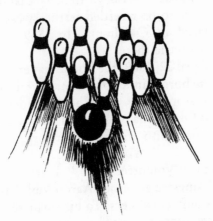

pure life. Its popularity spread from the cloisters to the general population of Germany and the Low Countries. The Dutch became especially fond of a version of the game using nine pins.

Bowling as we know it today evolved from this seventeenth-century Dutch game of ninepins. Early ninepins was played outdoors. By the early nineteenth century, there were several indoor bowling alleys in New York, and the game had a wide following along the Eastern Seaboard. Gambling on ninepins was very popular and the game was outlawed in some states, including Connecticut, in 1850. It is said that tenpins was then played as a way to circumvent the laws banning ninepins. Tenpins soon became more popular than ninepins and the game quickly spread throughout the United States.

Why do police hang their hats above the passenger side seat in their patrol cars?

They need room on the seat for doughnuts! While this may or may not be true, there is another reason. Not only is it a convenient place to hang their hat, two silhouettes are produced, making it appear that there are two police officers in the car at night.

This adds to the safety and security of the officer, as wrongdoers may be more wary of two policemen than of one.

Why do tree leaves change color in the autumn?

Chlorophyll is the dominant pigment in green plants and gives tree leaves their green color in the summer. Other pigments are also present but are masked by the abundant chlorophyll.

As the daylight shortens in autumn and the nights become cooler, deciduous trees "sense" the onset of winter and prepare to shed their leaves. They do this by sealing the leaves off from the vascular system of the tree. Deprived of water and nutrients, a leaf's chlorophyll breaks down and the green color fades while the yellow and orange pigments become more prominent.

Some leaves turn red and purple. This is due to the cold nights, which cause the breakdown of sugars and their conversion into red and purple pigmentation. The best autumn weather conditions for good leaf color are sunny days followed by clear, cool nights with temperatures below forty-five degrees Fahrenheit.

Because trees drop their leaves in autumn we call this season "fall."

Why do evergreens stay green all year round?

Trees lose their leaves to conserve moisture. On broadleaf trees water evaporates through their leaves. In warm months, water is usually available in the soil to replace this constant loss of moisture. In winter, however, when the soil can freeze solid, tree roots may be cut off from their water supply, causing the trees to dry up and die.

Evergreens have much smaller, thinner leaves or needles, and a thicker waxy cuticle, to cut down on evaporation. Hence, they do not have to shed all their leaves and their leaves do not change color. Pines and other evergreens do, however, shed their needles. They just don't do it all at once, as broadleaf trees do. Just look beneath a pine tree sometime. The ground will be covered with needles. Thankfully, evergreens do retain most of their leaves during the cold months, or winter would be that much drabber.

Why are diamonds measured in carats?

Gem diamonds are graded according to clarity, color, cut, and weight. Diamonds, however, are weighed in "carats." The word is derived, not from the orange vegetable, but from a bean. Precious stones were once weighed using the carob bean, which is produced by the tree *Ceratonia siliqua*. The bean was used because it is always the same weight, 0.2 grams. There are approximately 142 carats or carob beans in an ounce (28.35 grams). There are one hundred points to a carat, or .002 grams per point.

The largest diamond ever unearthed, known as the *Cullinan*, weighed a whopping 3,106 carats or about 1.3 pounds. It was found in 1905 in the Premier Mine of South Africa. The government of Transvaal purchased the *Cullinan* and presented it to King Edward VII of Britain. (During the nineteenth century, Transvaal was a Boer republic in South Africa.) The stone was sent to Amsterdam to be cut and polished. From it, nine large gemstones and ninety-eight smaller ones were created, including the largest cut diamond in the world. It is called the *Cullinan I* or *Star of Africa* and weighs 530 carats.

Diamond cutting and polishing techniques were developed during the fifteenth and sixteenth centuries. Early diamond cutters learned that certain diamond shapes resulted in greater brilliance than others. The style of cut most common today is the round shape, with fifty-eight facets, called the "brilliant cut." This cut causes most of the light entering a diamond to be reflected internally and emerge from the top. Most finished diamonds now have fifty-eight facets, thirty-three on the upper surface and twenty-five on the lower. The diameter of a diamond isn't always representative of its actual weight in carats. A diamond with a deeper cut will have a smaller diameter than one of the same weight with a shallower cut.

When is the flu not the flu?

Odds are that in the past year you have had a touch of what you may have thought was the flu or "a bug." Maybe you had a headache and a few days of diarrhea or vomiting. If you had intestinal problems, however, it probably was not the flu. The flu is a virus and its typical symptoms are more respiratory in nature with aching, fever, and breathing or sinus problems. Whether or not you realized it, it is more likely you had a case of food poisoning.

The main culprit of food poisoning is the bacterium *Salmonella enteritidis*. Each year, roughly one third of the U.S. population will get noticeable food poisoning (salmonellosis) and thousands will die from it. You may get several doses of mild food poisoning a year that you really don't notice.

Salmonella, as well as other bacteria, are found among the soil and feces where food animals are raised. But the animals can become infected and not show any symptoms. During processing the bacteria can be spread from animal to animal. These bacteria can be found in a host of animal food products, such as raw meats, poultry, fish, shellfish, eggs, and milk.

It may surprise you to know that your own house pets can also carry salmonella. Little Fluffy or Fido or Polly can be infected. This is the reason you can't buy those cute little department store turtles anymore. It was determined that 15 percent of all cases of salmonellosis were caused by these little devils, and the government banned their sale in 1971.

Incidentally, most cases of salmonellosis aren't caused by eating out, but are self-inflicted. The most common cause of salmonellosis in the United States is turkey, followed by beef and chicken. Turkeys, being large and usually sold frozen, are often undercooked. And beef is commonly eaten rare. This is why these two meats are the most dangerous. In order to thoroughly kill the bacteria, meat should be cooked to at least 170 degrees Fahrenheit.

Salmonellosis is quite different from common food poisoning, which is caused by *Staphylococcus aureus.* Staphylococcus food poisoning symptoms appear shortly after consumption and its toxins cause the body to purge itself through violent vomiting and diarrhea. Happily, it is usually over in a few hours. In contrast, *Salmonella* poisoning symptoms appear from several hours to a few days after the tainted food is consumed.

Since bacteria can multiply extremely rapidly, a small amount of them can spread rather quickly in unrefrigerated foods. By rapidly fanning out from one small spot in a food, such as a dip, they can contaminate one area of the dip but not another. Consequently, two people could eat out of the same bowl of dip and only one might get sick.

There are a few ways to protect yourself from home food poisoning. Keep your refrigerator setting below 40 degrees Fahrenheit; defrost foods in the fridge or microwave, not on a countertop; use different utensils and plates to handle meat after cooking, not the ones used for the meat before and during cooking. Salmonella can linger for months in your kitchen, on cutting boards, dishtowels, sponges, etc. Be sure to keep all these items spotless!

Why is the climate of Western Europe so mild compared to the other regions of the world on the same latitude?

England is at a higher latitude than most of Newfoundland, but has a much milder climate. This is due to ocean currents and winds. The prevailing winds in Western Europe blow off the North Atlantic. Oceans absorb and radiate heat more slowly than land masses do. Therefore, the ocean usually has a more moderate year-round temperature than does the adjacent land, which has temperature swings that closely follow the changes in air temperature. Add to this the fact that the warm Gulf Stream current flows north near the British Isles and you have a situation where warm winds blow inland off the Atlantic over Western Europe.

Cities like Chicago and New York, which are at much lower latitudes than England (Chicago is over five hundred miles farther south than London) have much more severe winter weather. Yet the average January temperature range for Chicago is from 14° F to 29° F; London's, 35° F to 44° F. Northwest Minnesota, which is farther south than London, has a mean January temperature of 1° F. London's mean January temperature is a balmy 43° F.

The prevailing winter winds in Chicago and Minnesota blow from the northwest out of Canada, bringing arctic blasts of cold air. Winds known as Alberta clippers blow from the province of Alberta, Canada, across the Great Lakes and the Northeast, bringing bitter cold. Alberta clippers generally are rapidly moving weather systems and don't bring much snow but occasionally they stall and create blizzard conditions.

Why do oysters make pearls?

Pearl oysters live on the sandy bottom of tropical seas. They filter the water to extract food. Any foreign matter (bits of sand or parasites) that invade their bodies can cause irritation. As a defense mechanism, oysters will coat a grain of sand with nacre, or mother-of-pearl, a silvery calcium carbonate substance that the oyster usually exudes to line its shell. After several years of coating, pearls are formed. Depending upon the pigments in the nacre, they can be white, pink, blue, yellow, or even black.

Pearl-producing oysters can be found in several areas of the world, including the Persian Gulf, the Red Sea, the Gulf of Manaar (between Sri Lanka and India), and the Great Barrier Reef. Perhaps the most well-known pearl-producing region is Japan, where the famous women divers (*ama*) risk their lives retrieving oysters. They dive as deep as forty feet and can stay down several minutes. Most divers today, however, use scuba gear.

In the early 1900s the Japanese learned how to cultivate pearls. This has been a boon to the pearl industry, as naturally occurring pearls are quite rare. It takes about one ton of oysters to find one good pearl.

By having their shells carefully opened and small bits of shell inserted as "seeds," oysters can be stimulated to produce market-size pearls in three to six years. And by using different-shaped seeds, pearls of a desired shape can be cultured. The exact Japanese techniques are closely guarded secrets. Attempts to culture pearls outside of Japan have met with limited success, but the culturing of freshwater pearls is being practiced in the United States.

Some freshwater mussels can also produce pearls. They are usually red or pink in color.

Due to the high cost of pearls, imitations abound. The better quality imitations are made out of nacre, shell, or coral. Cheap ones are made of glass beads coated with a solution of fish scales, known as "essence d'Orient." Imitations are smoother than real pearls and tend to lose their luster in time.

It may soon be possible to produce real pearls in the laboratory through genetic engineering with mantle tissue. Then the price of pearls should tumble, unless this new technique of culturing pearls is also kept a closely guarded secret, or worse yet, patented.

Why does Morton salt use the girl under the umbrella logo?

This logo has been around for decades. One problem with ordinary table salt (sodium chloride) is that it usually contains trace amounts of magnesium chloride, which causes it to become damp and clump together in the shaker during periods of wet weather. This problem is overcome by adding small quantities of sodium silicoaluminate to the salt.

The little girl walking in the rain has a box of Morton salt under her arm that is pouring out very nicely, implying that "when it rains, it pours," if you are using Morton Salt.

Why do people in India eat such spicy food?

Spicy food is a funny thing, either you love it or you hate it. Those of us who eat it think it is just wonderful—850 million Indians can't be wrong! Actually, they aren't. There are several good reasons why Indians and other people from hot climates eat spicy food.

The favored spice of India is curry, which is really a mixture of several spices, such as turmeric, cayenne, cardamom, ginger, coriander, pepper, chili, mustard seed, cumin, and cinnamon, among others.

Spices can make bland, unappealing food taste and smell better and improve one's appetite. This, however, is just one of the reasons why people add spices to foods. There are also other practical purposes for spice. Because spices, like curry, are "hot," they cause the body to sweat and thus help to regulate the body's temperature, making one feel cooler. For this reason, spicy foods are very popular in India, Mexico, and other warm countries. Spices in food also help to kill some germs and aid the digestive process.

Why are American space shots all launched from Cape Canaveral, Florida?

U.S. space shots have always lifted off from Cape Canaveral, Florida (also called Cape Kennedy for a while). The reason for this is purely scientific. Southern Florida is the most ideal location in the continental United States for launching rockets into space. A multistage rocket needs a vast expanse of ocean over which to take off. There is nothing but water for five thousand miles off Cape Canaveral, until you get to the coast of Africa.

Launching over the ocean allows the first two stages of the rocket to fall harmlessly to earth after they are detached. If they launched from the Midwest, the rocket's stages could fall on populated areas.

The reason the East Coast is preferable to the West Coast is due to the rotation of the Earth. The Earth rotates from west to east at a speed of 910 miles per hour. Rockets need to reach a speed of 17,300 miles per hour to enter orbit. Therefore, by launching in an easterly direction, the rocket already has a starting speed of 910 miles per hour while still on the launch pad and needs only to accelerate to about 16,450 miles per hour to reach orbit.

If, on the other hand, the rocket were launched to the west, it in essence would start at minus 910 miles per hour and would need to accelerate to about 18,200 miles per hour to achieve orbit, a difference of 1800 miles per hour.

Where did we get the names for the twelve months of the year?

The word calendar is from the Latin *kalendae*, meaning the day on which accounts are due. Our modern calendar takes the names of the months from the ancient Roman calendar. The original Roman calendar, created by Romulus, had only ten months. In 700 B.C., Numa Pompilius added January and February, to make twelve months. March was considered the first month of the year. The months obtained their names as follows:

January—Named for the Roman god Janus, who was the keeper of the gates of heaven. He had two heads, one facing backward to look at the old year and one facing forward to look ahead at the new year.

February—Named for the purification festival, Februa, when Romans prepared for the new year. It was the last month of the Roman year.

March—Named after the Roman god of war and agriculture, Mars. March is the traditional start of planting time.

April—Name comes from the Latin *aperire*, which means to open. It is in April when leaf and flower buds begin to open.

May—Named after the Roman goddess of growth in living things, Maia. It could also be derived from the Latin *Majores*, meaning "older men," because they were honored in May.

June—Named after the Roman goddess of marriage and childbirth, Juno, or after the Latin *Juniores*, meaning "young men," who were honored during June. It was, and still is, popular to marry during this month.

July—Named for Julius Caesar. After his assassination, Mark Antony renamed the fifth month of the Roman calendar (Quintilis), for Julius, because he was born during this month.

August—Named after Caesar Augustus. August was originally Sextillus, the sixth month of the Roman calendar. After Caesar Augustus became emperor, Sextillus was renamed in his honor. Sextillus was chosen because it was his "lucky month," in which he won a major military victory. At the time, August had only thirty days. This did not sit well with Augustus. July, named after his great-uncle, Julius, had thirty-one days. In order to make August as long as July, he stole a day from February and gave it to August. Thus, August has thirty-one days and February has only twenty-eight. Another reason for stealing a day was that the Romans considered even numbers unlucky and Augustus, like most Romans, was very superstitious.

September, October, November, and December—Their names came from the Latin words meaning seventh (*septem*), eighth (*octo*), ninth (*novem*), and tenth (*decem*), respectively. They are remnants of the early Roman year, which had only ten months. These names make no sense in our modern calendar, as they are now the ninth, tenth, eleventh, and twelfth months of the year.

Why is Australia considered a continent and Greenland an island?

There is really no guideline for differentiating between a continent and a big island. Geographers just decided that Australia should be a continent. In fact, Europeans consider the New World (North and South America) to be one continent, not two, because it is one land mass. Why they don't use the same logic and consider Europe and Asia to be one land mass and therefore one continent, is baffling.

If you look at a world map, Greenland appears to be as large as Australia. This, however, is an illusion created by flattening a three-dimensional (3-D) globe shape of Earth onto a two-dimensional (2-D) flat piece of paper.

Sixteenth-century sailors found it difficult to plot their courses on a chart because early maps did not take into account Earth's spherical shape. On Earth, the lines of longitude converge on the poles. A man named Gerardus Mercator (1512–1594) found a way to put segments of this sphere on a flat paper so that sailors could lay out their compass course by a straight line. Mercator imagined them on 2-D paper. To make the segments fit onto a flat square, the northernmost and southernmost regions had to be exploded or expanded to larger than their actual proportions. A map of this type is called a "Mercator projection." This is why Greenland and Antarctica look much larger on a map than they do on a globe.

Australia is actually three and a half times the size of Greenland. Australia contains 2,966,200 square miles. Greenland has "only" 840,000 square miles. Greenland is not really one big island, but is actually several smaller islands covered by a thick ice cap. Without its ice cap, Greenland's land area would be closer to 650,000 square miles.

Does lightning ever strike twice?

Always. Each bolt of lightning is really a succession of bolts that hits the same spot several times.

In thunderclouds a positive electrical charge builds in the upper part of the cloud, while a negative charge builds at the base. This negative charge causes a region of the ground beneath the cloud to become positively charged. This positive region follows the storm as it moves along and acts to attract the negative charge of the cloud. In contrast to what you may think, the cloud sends "leader" strokes down while the ground sends up electrically charged "streamers." When the two meet, the electrical pathway is completed. There is then a huge surge of power from the ground up into the clouds and an immediate return stroke of current to the ground. It is the return stroke that creates the flash we see as lightning. There are several return strokes between earth and sky that take place so quickly that we see them as one flash, although multiple strokes make the lightning bolt appear to flicker.

The electrical charge in the ground below a storm becomes more concentrated in high objects such as trees and buildings, and attracts leader strokes from the clouds. Skyscrapers can be hit by several bolts of lightning in a single storm.

A bolt of lightning may contain 15 million volts of electricity and can reach temperatures of fifty-four thousand degrees Fahrenheit, capable of turning soil to glass and vaporizing trees. This incredible heat, four times hotter than the surface of the sun, causes the air around it to expand rapidly, creating shock waves. These shock waves cause the booming we know as thunder.

There are more thunderstorms in central Florida, where

sea breezes hit coastal headlands, than anywhere else in the United States. Florida has about one hundred thunderstorms a year. The Midwest is second with about fifty thunderstorms a year.

Each year lightning kills about two hundred people in the United States and starts about nine thousand fires. There are some warning signs that lightning is imminent. If your hair begins to stand on end, your skin begins to tingle, or you hear clicking sounds, watch out! Lightning may be about to strike and you may be acting as a lightning rod. In open areas, it is best to crouch low and minimize your contact with the ground. Lying down is not a good idea as large amounts of current tend to concentrate at ground level near the point of a lightning strike, and a surface current may go through you.

There was a forest ranger named Roy C. Sullivan, of Virginia, who should have followed this advice. He was hit by lightning on seven different occasions between 1942 and 1977, and became known as the "lightning conductor of Virginia."

Golfers seem to be favorite targets of lightning. They walk around wide-open courses swinging metal clubs about in the air and will usually wait until the last possible moment before a storm to give up a game, or worse yet, play on under an umbrella.

In 1749, Benjamin Franklin invented the lightning rod, which was readily employed around the United States, except in New England, where God-fearing Puritans believed the rods interfered with the will of the Lord. But the invention of the lightning rod, which attracts a bolt of lightning above the roof of a building and conducts it harmlessly down a metal cable sunk into the ground, has saved thousands of lives.

It is possible to calculate how far away lightning is. Since light travels faster than sound, you can count the number of seconds that elapse between the flash of light and the sound of thunder, divide by five, and you will have the approximate distance of the storm, in miles, from where you are.

What's that little flap at the back of your throat?

It may remind you of a miniature punching bag, but it is actually called the uvula. It is small bit of muscle that hangs down from the back of the palate. This is what moves when you say "Ahhh!" for the doctor. The uvula flips up to cover the nasal passage when you swallow; however, you could swallow well without one. It is not really vital for talking or singing either. While medical experts may say that the uvula is not a vital structure, we would find it hard to gargle without one.

Why are basketball players called cagers?

In early days, basketball courts were surrounded by metal or cloth netting. This prevented the ball from going into the crowd. Perhaps more important, it also prevented obnoxious spectators from throwing objects at the players or officials. So, in essence, the game was played inside a cage. Thus, the players became known as cagers.

Why are piggy banks shaped like pigs?

Pigs have recently lost the stigma of being dirty, lazy creatures. Today, there is a pig mania sweeping the country. People are buying everything from calendars with a pig motif to miniature pigs as house pets. The creation of the piggy bank was, however, purely accidental, as many great creations are.

In ancient times a lump of clay was called *"pygg."* Clay bowls were fashioned from this pygg. People would keep

their coins in these bowls and they became known as pygg bowl banks. As the story goes, later in history an order was placed with a potter for several of these pygg bowl banks. The potter, unfamiliar with the term, made ceramic banks shaped like pigs. They were a hit and became known as piggy banks. It is only appropriate that some of the bacon we bring home is dropped into a bank shaped like a pig.

What popular beer has a hooker on its label?

The label of St. Pauli Girl beer has a buxom German beauty serving up six glass mugs of brew. St. Pauli Girl is named for the St. Pauli neighborhood of Hamburg, Germany, which was historically a red-light district. This leads one to believe that beer may not be the only thing that a St. Pauli girl might serve up.

Do you have skeletons in your closet?

Probably not. Not real ones anyway. This expression, meaning something in your past that you wish to keep hidden away, comes from Old England.

In the Middle Ages, not much was known about human

anatomy. Autopsies were occasionally performed after the Black Death plague of 1348, but dissections of human cadavers for purely scientific reasons occurred very rarely. Bodies of executed criminals served as the only source of legal cadavers. Women's bodies, however, were rarely used and usually cadavers were mutilated during executions and also missing various body parts. Lack of refrigeration made for hasty dissections. Even the best universities performed dissections only once or twice a year. To overcome this scarcity of human bodies, medical students had to steal bodies out of newly dug grave sites for study, or buy them on the black market. The grave-robbing business thrived in eighteenth-century England. Grave robbers became known as "resurrection men."

British law strictly prohibited surgeons from dissecting cadavers, except for those of executed criminals. The ill-gotten skeletons were usually thrown into rivers or fed to dogs. Skeletons were sometimes kept for future study, often locked away in closets, for possession of them was a punishable crime.

New Yorkers rioted for three days in April 1788 when they learned that the doctors at the Hospital of the City of New York were robbing graves. Subsequently, a law was passed in 1789 allowing doctors to legally obtain corpses for dissection.

Why do dim stars appear brighter when we don't look directly at them, but off to the side?

Next time you are out for an evening walk, take a look at a faint star. If you look directly at it, it may almost disappear. However, if you look off to one side, it will be much easier to see. The reason for this phenomenon lies in the anatomy of our eyes.

We have two types of light-sensitive cells in the retina—rods and cones. During daylight we use the color-sensitive cone cells that function well in bright light. At night our eyes switch to the color-blind rod cells, which are ten times more sensitive to light. Since these light-sensitive rod cells are arranged around the outside of the retina, we can see faint objects such as stars, more clearly, by looking a little to one side rather than looking directly at them.

Certain animals' eyes, like cats', are far more light-sensitive than are human eyes. Cats' eyes contain more rod cells and have a highly reflective layer of cells behind the retina. It is this layer, called the tapetum, that reflects light and makes cats' eyes appear to glow at night when light hits them.

Why is poison ivy poisonous?

Poison ivy, poison oak, and poison sumac are all members of the cashew family and cause contact dermatitis, or skin rash. Poison ivy produces an alcohol (catechol) that is stored within its plant tissue. Merely touching the leaves will cause no reaction. The leaves must be broken to release the allergin.

These plants evolved poisons to protect themselves from plant-eating animals, not just to ruin our camping trips.

If you wash your hands and other areas of the body within ten minutes of exposure, you can avoid an allergic reaction, as the allergin cannot penetrate the skin this quickly. However, wash with water alone, because soap removes protective oils from the skin.

In the United States, poison ivy and western poison oak are responsible for more clinical cases of dermatitis than all other plant and chemical sensitizers combined. Believe it or not, in California over 50 percent of all workmen's compensation cases are caused by poison oak–induced dermatitis. That's one itchy state!

What is the difference between fruits and vegetables?

What is a fruit? The answer depends on whether you ask a botanist or a culinary expert. Technically, a fruit is the mature, sexually produced seed-bearing ovary of a flowering plant. Vegetables come from the vegetative or nonsexual parts of the plant (leaves, roots, stems). So fruits include apples, oranges, nuts, and such seed-bearing "vegetables" as peas, beans, squash, eggplants, and tomatoes. The tomato is actually a berry, as is the pineapple. The various types of vegetables include roots (carrots and radishes), leaves (lettuce and spinach), flower buds (broccoli and cauliflower), and stems (rhubarb).

In the culinary world, tomatoes are considered a vegetable and rhubarb is considered a fruit. Nuts fall into a separate category.

Why is West Virginia so named, when Virginia actually extends ninety-five miles farther west?

West Virginia was a part of the Commonwealth of Virginia until 1861. The western counties of Virginia never much liked being subjected to the rules of the eastern part of the "state." At the start of the Civil War, in 1861, most of the counties of Virginia voted to secede from the Union. Forty of the more westerly counties voted to stay in the Union, and formed a new State, Kanawha, subsequently named West Virginia. It was admitted to the Union in 1863.

What makes one year of wine better than another?

There are four basic factors that help determine the quality of wine—the grape variety, the soil type, the grower, and the weather. The weather is the one big variable in wine making from year to year. The custom of marking the year a wine was grown on the label came about because in areas where the summers are unpredictable and cool, the year of vintage can be critical to the overall quality. In growing areas where the summer climate is usually hot, there will not be much variation in the grapes from year to year and the vintage year is not so important.

The ratings for wines of different years refer to the quality expected when the wine will be at its peak, anywhere from two to ten years after harvest.

Whom is the Mason-Dixon line named after?

The creation of the Mason-Dixon line had nothing to do with the Civil War. In fact, it was drawn when America was still a British colony. The line was established between 1763 and 1767 by English astronomer/surveyors Charles Mason and Jeremiah Dixon to settle a land dispute involving the William Penn family of Pennsylvania to the north and the Calvert family of Maryland to the south.

The border between Pennsylvania and Maryland was drawn as a straight line and represents the eastern portion of the Mason-Dixon line. The western portion, which continues west along the Ohio River to the Mississippi River, was completed in 1784. During the debates over the Missouri Compromise in 1820 and 1821, the line was used to separate the slave states and free states. During the Civil War it became a convenient line of reference separating the Union from the Confederacy. West Virginia, however, which stayed in the Union, fell south of the Mason-Dixon line.

The Mason-Dixon line is still used as an imaginary boundary between the "North" and the "South." Most of the original survey markers are still in place.

By the way, the word "Dixie" has nothing at all to do with the Mason-Dixon line. It is derived from the French word "dix," meaning "ten," which appeared on early banknotes in Louisiana. The name became popularized by the 1859 song "Dixie," by Dan Emmett.

Did Scotch tape originate in Scotland?

Its creation, here in the United States, was purely accidental. In 1926, the Minnesota Mining and Manufacturing Company (3M), tried to save a few bucks and started using a cheaper adhesive on their sticky tape. A Detroit automaker ordered some for use while spray painting autobodies. Apparently the automaker complained that the tape was "Scotch" (a derogatory word meaning cheap or stingy) in its stickum, which resulted in poor adhesion. While the tape didn't have the adhesion to satisfy this customer, it did have other suitable uses, as we all know; so the tape was kept and the name Scotch just "stuck." (Sorry for the cheap pun.)

If the moon is rotating, and Earth is rotating, why is the same side of the moon always facing Earth?

How many times have you looked at the moon on a clear night? Its size and shape varies, depending on what quarter it is in, but you will always see the same side. Even though the moon rotates on its axis, once every twenty-nine-and-a-half days, no one ever sees the dark side. The reason for this unusual fact is that the moon rotates on its axis at the same rate as it revolves around Earth. The Earth's gravity has locked the moon in this pattern and we always see the same familiar "man in the moon" face looking back at us.

Why do outhouses have half-moons on the door?

As you can well imagine, outhouses have been around since man first required a little privacy to answer nature's call. In times before the use of indoor plumbing, large segments of the population were illiterate, so the words "Men" or "Women" on an outhouse door to differentiate between the two was pointless. Therefore, simple commonly recognized symbols, the half-moon and the star, came to represent male and female outhouses, respectively. For whatever reason, the half-moon (actually a crescent-shaped moon) remains the traditional decorative symbol of outhouse doors.

Why do camels have humps?

No, it's not to store water, as commonly believed, although the camel can extract water from the hump. The camel has no layer of fat under its skin like most mammals. The hump is a large deposit of fat, weighing up to eighty pounds, that the camel can use for food and water in times of need. By breaking down the fat into hydrogen and oxygen, water is formed.

A camel can go for several days, even weeks, without water or food. When it does, its hump shrinks in size as its energy and water are used and tends to hang down on the animal's side. When a camel finally gets water, it can drink up

to thirty gallons at one time. Camels can eat almost anything they find growing in the desert, even cacti. Their mouths have extremely thick skin, which cactus needles cannot penetrate.

Speaking of humps, the dromedary, or Arabian camel, has only one hump; the Bactrian camel has two.

Why does inhaling helium from a balloon make your voice sound so funny?

Most of you have probably tried this old party trick at some time, much to the delight of yourselves and your friends. Little did you realize the simple property of physics which this "experiment" demonstrates.

The sound of your voice varies with its frequency. The higher the frequency of your voice, the higher the pitch it will have. The frequency of sound increases proportionally with its speed. This is why the pitch of an approaching train whistle is higher than one moving away. Since helium is lighter and less dense than air, sound travels faster through it than through air. When you replace the air in your lungs and mouth with helium and then speak, the sound of your voice is traveling faster than normal. Thus, its frequency and pitch are higher, and you sound like some kind of alien.

What is the origin of ketchup?

Ketchup has its roots in seventeenth-century China. In 1690, Chinese cooks developed a brine sauce of pickled fish, shellfish, and spices that they used on fish and fowl. They called the tangy sauce "ke-tsiap." This new sauce became popular and its use spread to Malaya, where it was called "kechop." In the early eighteenth century, English sailors traveling to Malaysia and Singapore bought the kechop and brought it home to England. English cooks tried to imitate the Chinese recipe, but lacking many of the Eastern ingredients, substituted mushrooms, walnuts, and cucumbers. The English called this concoction "ketchup."

Among the several varieties of ketchup they created were oyster, walnut, anchovy, lemon, and tomato. Its introduction to the United States came in 1792 when a recipe for tomato "catsup" was published in a cookbook. It didn't become widely popular in the United States until H. J. Heinz began mass producing it in 1876. (See pages 176–177, on Heinz 57 varieties).

Today, ketchup is made of tomatoes, vinegar, corn syrup, salt, and other natural flavorings—a far cry from the Chinese fish brine sauce. Whether you call it ketchup or catsup, over 500 million bottles of the stuff are sold each year in the United States.

Why does popcorn pop?

Popcorn (Zea mays everta) is a kind of corn called flint corn. It has small hard kernels that contain only a small amount of soft starch. Each kernel has a moisture content of about 13.5 percent. The kernels contain a food storage layer known as endosperm. This tough, elastic layer resists the build-up of steam pressure within the kernel when heated. When the temperature reaches a critical point, around four hundred degrees Fahrenheit, the endosperm violently ruptures as the contents of the kernel expand from thirty to thirty-five times their original size.

Popcorn is a relatively minor crop. It is grown primarily in Indiana, Illinois, Iowa, and Ohio. Unlike sweet corn, popcorn is harvested after it has matured and dried on the corn stalk. While dry, unsalted popcorn may taste like styrofoam, it has the same nutritional value as sweet corn.

Early American settlers were first introduced to popcorn by the Native Americans. The Colonists enjoyed their popcorn in milk and topped with sugar. This was probably the first American breakfast cereal.

Why is New Jersey called the Garden State?

New Jersey is the most densely populated and urbanized state in the nation. It is also, perhaps, the most maligned. If you travel anywhere in the country and tell people you come from New Jersey they are likely to ask you, "Which exit?" But the myth of New Jersey being wall-to-wall concrete is erroneous. New Jersey has almost two million acres of forestland.

New Jersey or Jersey, as the locals call it, is situated between two of the largest cities in the nation, New York City and Philadelphia. There is a great demand for fresh produce in their markets. New Jersey, in its earlier history, had a great number of produce farms and still does today. As of 1990 there were 8,300 farms in New Jersey comprised of approximately 850,000 acres of land. Many of these farms specialize in produce which is easily trucked into the nearby cities on the state's extensive highway system. (These are known as truck farms.) There is virtually no place in the state that is more than twenty miles from a major multilane highway.

New Jersey is especially famed for its vine-ripened Beefsteak tomatoes and Silver Queen corn. New Jersey is also one of the country's top producers of blueberries, cranberries, and peaches. Aside from commercial agriculture, there are uncounted numbers of home gardens of all types.

So, if you ever find yourself in New Jersey, get off any exit and take a look around, you might be pleasantly surprised.

What does the Rx seen on pharmacy signs stand for?

This is not a registered trademark or a logo for some organization. The Rx symbol has been used by pharmacies and apothecaries for centuries. It is of Latin origin, as are many of the names of the drugs we buy. The R stands for *recipere,* which means "to take" in Latin. The little x, which is not separate from the R, but is a diagonal line through the leg of the R, represents the Roman god for medicine, Jupiter. The symbol is pronounced *ar-ex.*

How do meat tenderizers work?

Meats are composed of protein molecules. When meat is cooked, its large protein molecules are broken down. The connective tissue polymers combine with water and form smaller molecules that are easier for us to digest.

Meat tenderizers are made up of enzymes that chemically break down meat proteins, similar to the way cooking does. A naturally occurring enzyme found in papayas, papain, is used in some tenderizers. So, when you add tenderizers to your meat, you are actually kind of precooking it at room temperature.

Why are beer and soda sold in six-packs?

Standard twelve-ounce cans and bottles of beer and soda are traditionally sold in packages of six, or multiples thereof. Why is the number six and not four or five or some other number?

A brewer's main goal is to sell beer in multiple units. There is nothing special about the number six. Over the years all different numbers have been tried.

Supposedly, the first major brewer to promote six-packs was Ballantine in the late thirties. People, for some reason, just seemed to prefer buying packs of six. One reason for this may be that after Prohibition, women began buying the household beer while doing the family shopping. Packs of eight or ten weren't as easy for them to handle, so six-packs caught on. Coca-Cola was also sold in six-packs at that time and helped predispose people to buying beer that way.

Of course, eight-packs of beer in the smaller eight-ounce

bottles are also now available, as are four-packs of wine coolers. Odd numbers will probably never catch on.

Why are teddy bears so named?

Those cuddly, soft teddy bears we all grew up with were named after one of our roughest, toughest presidents, Teddy Roosevelt. Roosevelt was an avid sportsman and hunter. While out hunting one day in Mississippi, in 1902, he refused to shoot a bear cub that had been run down by his dogs, knocked out, and tied to a tree by the hunting party. This act of compassion was captured in a cartoon by Clifford Berryman and appeared in newspapers, catching the public's fancy.

Stuffed toy versions of the cute little cub spared by Roosevelt soon appeared in stores and were rapid sellers internationally. One story has it that these toy bears were given their name by two storekeepers in Brooklyn, Rose & Morris Michtom, who asked Roosevelt for permission to use his name, and that he graciously agreed. (Morris Michtom later went on to found the gigantic Ideal Toy Corporation.) They became known as teddy bears, the name by which they are still called today. The original teddy bear had a low forehead, a long nose, and wore a muzzle. Today's teddy bears have larger foreheads and shorter noses, features that make them look more human than bearlike.

Luckily for the little bear cub, he wasn't a year or two older or Teddy might have used him for a rug in the White House. Roosevelt may have liked hunting, but his love of the outdoors led him to become a leading advocate of the conservation movement to help protect vast areas of our country's wildlands for future generations.

What is a best boy, key grip, and gaffer?

For some reason, Hollywood producers feel it's necessary to recognize every person who is even remotely involved with the making of a movie; witness the endless, boring list of credits at the end of a film. When an author writes a book, he doesn't feel compelled to thank everyone who got him a coffee and doughnut during its creation or tell what kind of word processor paper was used for the manuscript!

For those of you interested enough to watch the closing credits, you will notice persons with strange-sounding titles, such as gaffer, key grip, and best boy. Hollywood has its own jargon, which sounds a little weird to outsiders. The gaffer is the chief electrician. The key grip is responsible for constructing or dismantling sets and also for laying the tracks upon which the cameras run. Supposedly, a strong grip is useful in these tasks. The best boy is the assistant to the gaffer and the key grip.

What is the origin of the Baby Ruth candy bar's name, and other popular food products' names?

Baby Ruth bars are not named for baseball great Babe Ruth as most people believe. They were created in 1920 by a young Chicago entrepreneur named Otto Schnering. Working out of a small rented room above a plumber's shop, he formed the Curtiss Candy Company and began developing one candy after another. For several years the company struggled to survive. But with the creation of the log-shaped Baby Ruth bar, Curtiss hit the jackpot. The candy, originally called Kandy Kate, was actually named for Ruth Cleveland, baby daughter of former president Grover Cleveland, who had been the nation's darling as an infant. "Baby Ruth," as she was affectionately known, was born on October 3, 1891, and tragically died on January 7, 1904. Babe Ruth had just joined the New York Yankees when the candy was created, but had not yet become a superstar.

Life Savers—Life Savers were invented in 1912 by Cleveland, Ohio, candymaker Clarence Crane. Summer was a bad time for makers of chocolate candy (in the time before air conditioning) as it tended to melt in your hand. Therefore, candy sales would decrease during the hot season. In order to beat the summer lull, Crane decided to create a hard confection that stayed fresh and appealing regardless of the weather, and he came up with a peppermint candy. Other mints of the time were square and pillow shaped. In order to differentiate his candies, he made them round with a hole in the middle. Their resemblance to miniature life preservers was obvious and a new candy name was born. Between 1913 and 1987, 33.4 billion were sold!

Lorna Doone shortbread cookies—Introduced in 1912, the cookie was named for Lorna Doone, the British heroine of a novel written by Richard Blackmore. They were used to make little "shortcake" sandwiches by putting a fruit or jelly between them.

Brand's A.1. steak sauce—The origin of A.1. goes back to the court of King George IV of England, circa 1820. His Majesty asked the royal chef to create a special steak sauce for him. The chef went to the royal kitchen and experimented with different mixtures of the royal spices and sauces. When he presented his new sauce to the king, George was very pleased and proclaimed the sauce to be "A-One." The sauce became very popular in England and was introduced to the commoners of the United States in 1906.

Barnum's Animals Crackers—Nabisco Animal crackers, also known as Barnum's Animals Crackers, were based on a design created in England in the late nineteenth century. The name of P. T. Barnum, the greatest showman, was used to promote the crackers when they debuted in 1902 in the United States. The small rectangular box, picturing a circus cage filled with animals, was very appealing to children, as was the string handle. The handle was not intended to be used for carrying the box, but was for parents to hang the boxes on Christmas trees as presents. We all enjoyed Animal Crackers as children or adults, but how many of us know the number of different kinds of animals that can be found in the circus box? Actually, there are seventeen: bears (sitting and walking), bison, camel, cougar, elephant, giraffe, gorilla, hippopotamus, hyena, kangaroo, lion, monkey, rhinoceros, seal, sheep, tiger, and, finally, a zebra.

Oreo cookies—Oreos were introduced in 1912 by the National Biscuit Company (N.B.C.) and were first sold as the Oreo Biscuit. It became the Oreo Sandwich in 1921, the Oreo Creme Sandwich in 1948, and the Oreo Chocolate Sandwich Cookie in 1974. No one knows for sure how the name Oreo came to be. One commonly accepted explanation is that the word may be derived from the French word "or" meaning gold. The original package label had gold scroll-work on a pale green background, while the product name was in gold. Another theory is that Oreos derive their name from the Greek word for "hill," because they were originally mound-shaped.

Oreos are still imprinted with the original symbol of the National Biscuit Company, an oval surmounted by a cross with two horizontal lines instead of the one. The first chairman of N.B.C., Adolphus Green, discovered this symbol late one night while thumbing through an old book of Italian printers' symbols. It was supposed to represent the triumph of good over evil. The Oreo cookie was good indeed to N.B.C., becoming the best-selling cookie in the world today. Over 200 billion have been sold so far. If stacked one on top of the other, they would stretch to the moon and back three times over!

Blue Bonnet margarine—During World War II, butter was in short supply. In 1942 Standard Brands Inc., which had just purchased the Standard Margarine Company of Indianapolis, decided to add margarine to its Fleischmann's butter product list. The company sponsored a contest to name the new margarine. A Standard Brands employee in Texas suggested the name of the Texas state flower, the bluebonnet. It was the winning entry. The company however, did not use a bluebonnet flower for the logo but opted to use a blond woman wearing a blue bonnet.

Log Cabin syrup—was named by a grocer, P. J. Towle, in

146

honor of his favorite president, Abraham Lincoln, who was born in a log cabin.

Why do military uniforms often have buttons up the cuff of the sleeve?

According to legend, the answer dates back to the time of Napoleon. The emperor was quite a snappy dresser and a perfectionist when it came to the appearance of his men. One of his pet peeves was the sight of soldiers wiping their noses on the sleeves of their uniforms. To discourage this nasty habit, he had large buttons sewed onto the uniform sleeves.

Did you ever try to wipe your nose on a sleeve full of brass buttons? Not a pleasant experience, but still preferable to a trip to the guillotine for disobeying orders.

What causes hiccups?

A hiccup is an involuntary contraction or twitching of the diaphragm; as air is inhaled, the space between the vocal cords closes, violently producing that annoying hiccup sound. Hiccups usually occur from eating or swallowing too fast or from some other irritation of the nerves that control the diaphragm.

There are dozens of so-called "remedies" for hiccups, many of which try to shock the nervous system to restore normal diaphragm motion or by reducing oxygen intake. Some include drinking a glass of water quickly while standing on the head, pulling the tongue and holding the nose, holding the breath, breathing into a paper bag, or a sudden scare.

Here is a "cure" that is said to work well: Swallow a heaping teaspoonful of granulated sugar, sit down, take a few deep breaths and totally relax your body, keeping your eyes closed and your breathing shallow. Within a few minutes you should feel fine.

What are those "highway mirages" or wet patches you keep seeing on the road ahead of you as you drive?

As you drive along on a hot, sunny day, it sometimes appears that there are puddles on the road ahead of you. As you approach them they disappear, and new ones appear farther ahead. Everyone can see them, so you know that you are not crazy, but no one seems to know what they are.

These mirages occur when a layer of hot air rising off the road is trapped by a layer of cooler air from above. The differing densities of the two air layers causes a disturbance of air molecules between the layers, which acts to reflect light from the sky and surroundings, thus causing a wet, mirrorlike appearance. Solar energy is absorbed by road surfaces on warm sunny days. Since air is a poor conductor of heat, the air in contact with the road is very hot, while the air a few feet above the road is much cooler. Blue sky light is refracted up into our eyes as it travels through air of different densities, causing the "puddles" to appear. The shimmering effect of these mirages is due to the constantly changing density of air that rises and falls.

Similar mirages appear on the desert. Many thirsty desert travelers have been disappointed to find that what appeared to be a refreshing pool of water turned out to be just more hot sand. It's enough to drive one mad from thirst and frustration.

So when you see these mirages on the road, don't worry, you are not crazy, but if you start seeing a cold can of beer up ahead . . .

What is the story behind the unique Procter & Gamble corporate trademark?

Established in 1837, Procter & Gamble began as a small soap and candle company in Cincinnati, Ohio. The original Procter & Gamble trademark first appeared around 1851 as a logo for Star Brand Candles, an early Procter & Gamble product. The design consisted of a man-in-the-moon face looking over a field of thirteen stars. The stars symbolized the thirteen original colonies. The man in the moon was a popular decorative fancy of the time.

In the 1860s the company tried to eliminate the logo as their trademark. A merchant rejected a shipment of star candles that carried a new trademark. He wrote the company a letter, scolding them for sending him an imitation product. This prompted the company to return to the man-in-the-moon logo. They registered this trademark in 1882.

A minor controversy erupted recently over the use of the trademark. Some misguided people believed that the logo represented Satan or Satan worship, or some such nonsense. This caused the company some concern and the trademark was removed from certain products. The moon and stars design, however, is still found on several product packages and is still proudly displayed both inside and outside of Procter & Gamble facilities.

What is the difference between decaffeinated and caffeine-free?
(and other information about caffeine)

Several beverages that we drink are labeled either decaffeinated or caffeine-free. Caffeine is a naturally occurring drug that is found in coffee, tea, and cola drinks. Colas do not have naturally high levels of caffeine. It is added by the bottlers to give it a little "zip" and to help hook you on its mildly addictive properties. Colas, therefore, are labeled caffeine-free when they contain very little or no caffeine. The caffeine is artificially added. Coffee and tea on the other hand, are labeled decaffeinated, meaning the caffeine is artificially removed. However, decaffeinated coffees do contain some caffeine, usually at least 2 percent.

The first decaffeinated coffee was Sanka, which is a contraction of the French *sans caffeine*. For years all decaffein-ated coffee was called Sanka, regardless of its brand. The process of removing caffeine was discovered by accident, when a shipment of coffee beans became soaked with seawa-ter during an ocean trip and was found to have had some of the caffeine removed. Today coffee is also decaffeinated by using water and carbon dioxide to extract the caffeine from the green coffee beans before roasting or by using chemical solvents.

A cup of brewed coffee contains up to 180 milligrams (mg) of caffeine. Instant coffee contains roughly two-thirds as much, and teas even less. A soft drink like Coca-Cola contains 46 mg in a twelve-ounce serving and Pepsi-Cola, 36.4 mg in twelve ounces. Surprisingly, noncola soft drinks such as Mountain Dew and Mello Yello contain 54 mg and 52 mg of caffeine, respectively; more than colas.

Caffeine is also used in aspirins and acetaminophens to enhance their painkilling abilities. Excedrin, for example, contains 65 mg of caffeine per tablet. When you ingest caffeine, its full effects are felt within fifteen to forty-five minutes. After five or six hours, half the caffeine in an adult's blood stream is gone. Children metabolize it at twice this rate.

The best time of day to have a cup of tea or coffee, is, oddly enough, "tea time," around four or five in the afternoon, as the British have done for centuries. Caffeine belongs to the class of stimulants called methylxanthines, which block the action of chemicals in the body that act as natural sedatives. Having a cup of coffee in the morning will give you a temporary boost, but upsets your biological clock, making you feel sleepy during the day. The caffeine raises your blood sugar levels for about an hour and a half. Then the body reacts by producing insulin, which is a natural sedative, to lower your blood sugar levels, causing you to feel a letdown. Your body's internal clock is peaking around 4:00 P.M. and a cup of coffee at this hour will do the most to charge you up without throwing your body's cycle out of kilter.

It is not recommended that the average person drink more than five cups of coffee a day, as excessive amounts of caffeine can cause restlessness, trembling, and palpitations, not to mention many trips to the bathroom.

Why do we have Sunday "blue laws"?

Blue laws or Sunday laws are government imposed restrictions on the sale of certain products or services on Sundays. They have their origins in early colonial American legislation requiring puritanical standards of Sunday observance on the part of the general public. Blue laws were the first printed laws of the New Haven Colony in Connecticut. They are called blue laws because they were originally bound in blue paper.

The first "Sunday" laws in what is now the United States, were enacted in Virginia in 1617. They called for the punishment of persons failing to attend Sunday church services, with a fine payable in tobacco. The Virginia militia was authorized to force colonists to attend Sunday Anglican church services.

Other colonial blue laws included the prohibition of work, travel, or recreation on Sundays, as well as many other restrictions, including such mundane activities as cooking, shaving, cutting hair, sweeping, and making beds. It was also illegal to have sexual intercourse on the Sabbath. The Puritans believed that a child was born on the same day of the week as it was conceived. Therefore, a woman who bore a child on a Sunday was fined for violating the blue law nine months earlier. In fact, mothers were forbidden to kiss their children on Sundays!

New York State punished blue law violators with a fine of six shillings and eight pence or two hours in the stocks.

Massachusetts law even forbade men and women from wearing lace or precious metals on Sundays.

In the nineteenth century, laws requiring Sunday church attendance began to disappear because they "violated citizens' rights to religious freedoms." The other restrictions, however, including those banning sporting events and travel, continued. The courts ruled the laws were constitutional because Sunday observance was a civil institution. As late as 1893, a New York man was convicted in court for fishing in a private lake on a Sunday. By the early twentieth century, prohibitions on Sunday travel were generally lifted.

Today, some of these laws still exist on state and local levels. Each state, county, and town has its own ideas of what we should be permitted to do on Sunday. Most states still do not allow the sale of liquor on Sunday. The holding of sporting or theatrical events which would conflict with church services is generally prohibited. Many states who still have laws prohibiting nonessential labor, trade, or business on the Sabbath, however, also have rules allowing persons who observe another day of the week for religious practice to work on Sundays. These laws vary widely from place to place and are maintained by local option.

The courts in New York and Connecticut recently had the good sense to declare blue laws unconstitutional. In theory, there is supposed to be a separation of church and state in America. Since blue laws were created and propagated by religious groups, their existence was declared unconstitutional by New York and Connecticut.

Why do baseball managers wear uniforms?

As any sports fan knows, baseball managers and coaches always wear the team uniform to games. Coaches in other sports wear suits or casual clothes. Is there a reason for baseball's unusual custom?

According to major league rules, only uniformed persons

are allowed on the playing field. Therefore, if a baseball manager wants to go to the mound to talk to his pitcher, he must be in uniform, as must all baseball coaches. The famous manager Connie Mack, however, wore suits to games. He had to stay in the dugout and let his coaches do the walking.

Thankfully, professional basketball coaches do not have this rule. Can you picture Pat Riley parading around courtside wearing silk shorts and a tank top?

Why do cats insist on rubbing themselves up against you and your furnishings?

Who says cats aren't friendly? They seem to be constantly rubbing themselves up against your legs in that lovable manner of theirs. This is far from being expression of pure affection; cats have an ulterior motive for their caressing. Through glands in their faces cats are actually depositing scents on you that mark you, as a warning for other cats that you are their property. Your cat's scent tells other cats that you and your furniture are taken and they need not apply.

Cats are, by nature, solitary animals, loners, who have little need for the affection or the pleasing of other cats. Dogs, on the other hand, are pack animals who in the wild live in a very organized social hierarchy where all the dogs rely on one another and must cooperate to survive. Dogs lower down on the totem pole must serve and please the more superior dogs. This need to be social and to please makes dogs more friendly, affectionate, and obedient pets.

Sorry, cat lovers, dogs really are the more social animals. Don't take it personally, it is perfectly natural.

Why does the moon appear to be larger when low on the horizon, as opposed to high in the sky?

The key word here is appear. The moon, optically, is the same size when low on the horizon as it is when high in the sky. An optical illusion is caused by the eye's errant visual perception. When just above the skyline, there are distant objects, trees, buildings, and mountains to compare the moon to and give it a sense of size and distance, or perspective. On the other hand, when it is high in the wide-open sky, we have no points of reference for the size and distance of the moon, and it seems dwarfed by the vast open space.

If you don't believe this, try a simple test. Outstretch your arm and extend your little finger while looking at the "large" rising moon. Compare its size to your fingernail. Later in the evening, when the "smaller" moon is high in the sky, measure it again with your fingernail. It should be the same size; if it isn't, have your eyes checked.

What is Fahrvergnügen?

During the late 1980s and early 1990s, it was impossible to sit down and watch a little television or open a magazine without seeing the word "Fahrvergnügen." It became part of the latest Volkswagen advertising campaign. Although Fahrvergnügen is a really neat-sounding word, VW doesn't actually explain what it means, if anything. Is it a real word or simply a European-sounding marketing word created by some German advertising executive?

Volkswagen's present-day slick advertising and stylish-looking European autos had much humbler beginnings in prewar Germany.

In 1934, car designer Ferdinand Porsche was directed by the Nazi government to create a small "peoples-car" or Volks-wagen. His new creation, the "Beetle," was introduced in 1939. The rear-engined, air-cooled, simple, and inexpensive little car quickly became one of the most popular cars ever produced. By 1972 the Volkswagen Beetle topped the Model-T in total sales, with over 15 million sold, and became the best-selling car of all time.

The truly remarkable thing about the Beetle was that relatively few changes were made over the years, and its basic design stayed the same. The Beetle model was discontinued in the United States in 1977, when it was replaced by the model called the Rabbit. The Beetle, however, still continues to be produced in Mexico and total sales have surpassed the $20 million mark.

In the late 1980s VW's marketing philosophy began to change and they introduced finely engineered European models that were more fun to drive. In order to present this new image to the American consumer, the company came up with a new advertising word—"Fahrvergnügen." Volkswagen's advertising agency, while seeking something unusual, catchy, and meaningful, came across the word "Fahrvegnügen" in a VW engineering manual at the Wolfsburg, Germany, factory complex. While the word literally translates into "the pleasure of driving" (from the German "fahr," meaning drive and "vergnügen," meaning pleasure), the engineers were using it to describe what they called the VW "fingerprint"..."that unique sense of control and road feel that the driver experiences behind the wheel of a Volkswagen."

Whether or not VW cars do indeed have Fahrvergnügen, you will have to judge for yourself. The company must be doing something right, however. Volkswagen is now the fourth-largest maker of cars in the world. Not bad for a company that had its humble beginnings producing the buglike "peoples-car" in prewar Germany.

Why do some people get freckles?

While some people consider freckles to be unsightly, they actually look quite charming on many people. Anyone can develop freckles, but they are most commonly found on fair-skinned people. As you would probably have guessed, the tendency to freckle is hereditary.

Freckles are nothing more than concentrated areas of pigment in the skin. The pigment, melanin, is the same one that causes the skin to tan when exposed to direct sunlight. Most light-skinned people don't tan very easily; they tend to burn. When exposed to sun, fair skin tans unevenly. The pigments can form irregular patterns of little brown spots, causing freckles. Between freckles the skin is likely to burn, due to lack of pigment.

The reason hair bleaches in the sun, instead of tanning, is because hair is dead and contains no melanin as living skin cells do. Whether or not evenly tanned skin is actually just one big freckle is another matter.

Why do flocks of geese fly in the familiar "V" pattern?

Unlike most other birds, which fly in apparently helter-skelter flocks, geese fly in an organized V-shaped arrangement. As you may have guessed, a deliberate and coordinated group action such as this obviously has a purpose. If you guessed that it increases aerodynamics, you are right. Geese are rather large and have to fight more air resistance than smaller birds. They are also long-distance fliers, traveling thousands of miles on their annual migrations. Therefore, increased group aerodynamics is very beneficial to the individual bird, as well as the gaggle.

The lead bird in the V pattern does the most work. He cuts the air ahead. As he flaps his wings down, he creates an upward current of air immediately behind him, which the birds following in the V can ride. They, in turn, create an updraft behind them. Each bird in line benefits from the wingbeats of those in front. The poor lead bird isn't stuck with the job, however. Every so often another bird moves up to take his place—hopefully one who has made the trip before.

Why do we call 12:00 P.M. "noon"?

Only two hours of the day have their own name—midnight and noon. The name midnight makes sense, as it comes about midway between sunset and sunrise. Noon, however, is a derivation of the Latin word *nono*, which means nine. But, you say, noon is at twelve o'clock, not nine o'clock! Right you are, but if the hours of the day were counted from sunrise (6:00 A.M.), the middle of the day, noon, would be at 3:00 P.M. Sometime around the 1400s noon came to mean midday or 12:00 P.M.

What is the last day of the twentieth century?

It may surprise you to learn that the twentieth century will end on December 31, 2000, not December 31, 1999. The twenty-first century won't start until January 1, 2001.

This curious situation is the result of the fact that there was no year A.D. 0 or 0 B.C. The Christian era began with the year A.D. 1; the year before that was 1 B.C. So the first century ended at the beginning of the year A.D. 101; ergo, the twentieth century will end at the beginning of the year 2001.

Why is Washington, D.C., the capital of the United States?

The site of the capital of the United States was moved several times during the Revolutionary War. Wherever the Continental Congress met was considered to be the capital at that time. Threatening British troops and regional jealousies caused the capital to be moved to several different locations, including Philadelphia, Pennsylvania; Baltimore, Maryland; New York, New York; Lancaster, Pennsylvania; Princeton,

New Jersey; Annapolis, Maryland; and Trenton, New Jersey. Several colonies, including Virginia, New Jersey, New York, and Maryland, proposed having the permanent capital established within their boundaries. Congress addressed the issue in 1783, ignoring all proposals and proclaiming that any site of the national government would be a "federal district" under the direct control of Congress and not a part of any particular colony or state.

It wasn't until 1788 that the Constitution was ratified, officially giving the Confederation a national government. Rivalries between the northern and southern states over where to locate the capital flared up in 1789. Northern delegates to Congress wanted Philadelphia, New York, or Germantown, Pennsylvania (near Philadelphia). The southern delegates pressed for a capital on the eastern banks of the Potomic River, the geographical center of the United States. George Washington also favored this site, as it was close to his home in Mount Vernon. John Adams cast the deciding vote in the Senate for Germantown, Pennsylvania. This caused much heated debate and there was even talk of secession.

While the north won this Congressional battle, the south won another. Secretary Alexander Hamilton had drafted the Assumption Bill, which would have the national government assume the war debts of the states. The northern states were keen on this bill since they had a greater war debt than the southern states. The southern states, however, did not want federal money to pay for northern debts and they controlled enough votes to kill the bill. Then Hamilton came up with a great compromise.

In closed negotiations with southerner Thomas Jefferson, the two men agreed that in return for enough southern votes to pass the Assumption Bill, the North would concede the capital site to the Potomac. On July 16, 1790, President Washington chose the site and pursuaded some area landowners to sell their property to the government to supplement the six hundred acres of land given by Virginia.

The site selected by President Washington for the capital was a curious one. This area of the Potomac was called "Foggy Bottom." It was basically swampland. When Congress moved to Washington, they felt as if they were in a great morass. The early nickname of the capital became "The Great Serbonian Bog." Sometimes it seems as though Washington's politicians are still lost in the mire. The city was named for the president. On June 3, 1800, President John Adams moved to Washington, and on June 10, 1800, Philadelphia ceased being the seat of the government. The City of Washington was incorporated in 1802. The District of Columbia was created as a municipal corporation in 1871, and included Georgetown, Washington, and Washington County.

What is the origin of the archaic American system of measurement?

While the rest of the world has converted to the orderly base-ten International (Metric) System, the United States still clings to the archaic U.S. "customary system" of measurement. Its origin is derived from the old British imperial system of measurement.

The history of measurement goes back thousands of years. Units of measure were set by several different individuals and methods over the years, none of which were connected in any logical mathematical way.

For example, the Romans set the measurement of the mile as the distance a soldier could march in one thousand double steps (about 5000 feet), not exact by any means. Queen Elizabeth I of England proclaimed in 1575 that the length of a mile should be increased to 5,280 feet, so that it could be evenly divided (eight times) by the furlong (660 feet), which was the length of a plowed furrow in an ordinary field.

The Emperor Charlemagne was vain enough to decree that a foot would be the length of his own foot. In fourteenth-century England, the foot was standardized to the length of thirty-five barley corns laid end to end. King Henry I established the size of a yard to be the distance from his nose to his extended fingertips. An inch was the length of a man's thumb from tip to first joint. A fathom was the length from fingertip to fingertip of the outstretched arms of a Viking. An acre was the amount of land a pair of oxen could plow in one day. Eventually, all these measures became standardized.

Today, 95 percent of the world uses the metric system. It was established during the French Revolution, by the French National Assembly. They decreed that the meter was to be one ten-millionth of the length of a line of longitude from the equator to the North Pole. Surveyors determined this distance to be 39.37 inches. The other metric units were derived from this length as factors of ten. Seven basic units comprise the metric system: time, second; mass, kilogram; length, meter; electric current, ampere; thermodynamic temperature, kelvin; amount of substance, mole; and luminous intensity, candela.

The United States was supposed to have converted to the metric system, but it never came to be. Most Americans are quite comfortable with our awkward yet familiar system and are resistant to change. The U.S. auto industry has gone metric to compete with foreign companies. Some industries inexplicably use a split system. For instance, Coca-Cola is sold in glass bottles by the pint (sixteen ounces) and in plastic bottles by the liter. Banks display the temperature in degrees Celsius (which everyone disregards), and Fahrenheit. The one segment of American society that has totally embraced the metric system is the scientific community, including the medical and pharmaceutical industries. They are pragmatists who realize the American system is cumbersome and obsolete.

For those of you who would prefer to see wider acceptance of the International System in the United States, take heart. The Trade Act of 1988 called for the federal government to adopt metric specifications by December 31, 1992. Don't hold your breath! Convincing Americans to actually learn and use the metric system still seems like wishful thinking.

Why do we use AC current instead of DC current?

But for the action of a few men in America's past, we might all be using direct current in our homes today. If Thomas Edison had had his way, this indeed would be the case.

As we all know, Edison invented the light bulb. His one major problem was what kind of filament to use. He tried hundreds of materials, including platinum, iridium, nickel, coconut hair, and carbon, with varying degrees of success. Most of these filaments melted or burned up. In late 1879, he tried charred cotton thread, which burned successfully for 13½ hours. He successfully increased the length of burning time by using carbonized cardboard, carbonized paper, and finally carbonized bamboo. The next obstacle to the widespread use of electric light was supplying electric power to the masses.

Edison had been using Alessandro Volta's simple direct current (DC) batteries. In direct current, electrons flow in one direction only, from a negative source to a positive terminal. To supply large quantities of electricity, a dynamo, or generator, was employed. Edison's generator provided direct current. By the 1880s European Nikola Tesla, among others, had developed motors that made use of alternating current (AC), so called because the electron flow changes directions sixty times a second. The terminals of supply repeat alternately from negative to positive and vice versa.

Tesla worked briefly for Edison before striking out on his own. He became the main proponent for AC; Edison was for DC. Thus began the great "Battle of the Currents."

George Westinghouse bought the rights for Tesla's AC motors. The two men worked to develop an efficient AC network for commercial use. AC had one big advantage over DC—it could be transmitted at high voltage over long distances and then be "stepped down" to lower voltages, by transformers, for domestic use. Low-voltage DC could only be transported for short distances.

Edison was adamantly opposed to the use of AC. He had huge investments in DC. By 1886, nearly sixty Edison power companies were operating with DC, so he set out to discredit AC. Edison stooped so low as to misinform the public about the safety of AC. He launched a campaign to convince consumers that AC kills. Edison and his cohorts staged several public demonstrations where animals were put to death by electrocution. When New York State adopted the use of electrocution for its death penalty, Edison tried to have a Westinghouse AC generator installed in Auburn State Prison, so that he could refer to AC as the "executioner's current." Since Westinghouse wouldn't supply an AC generator to Auburn, an Edison stooge arranged for a South American company to buy one and have it resold to the prison. The unfortunate man to be used as the human guinea pig for the electric chair was condemned killer Willie Kemmler. Prison authorities had to let the 1,700-volt current flow through Kemmler's body for a full eight minutes before they could be sure he was dead. This spectacle caused a public uproar, and convinced people that AC wasn't all that deadly if it took eight minutes to kill a man.

To further dispel the AC myth, the eccentric Tesla would pick up light bulbs and illuminate them, without wires, by letting high-frequency current travel through his body. AC won a major battle over DC when, by underbidding Edison, Westinghouse was awarded the lighting contract for the 1893 Chicago World's Fair. Here Tesla showed AC's versatility in powering both high-voltage heavy-duty equipment and low-voltage domestic appliances. The final blow to DC came in 1893 when Westinghouse and General Electric, using AC current, were chosen by J. P. Morgan and William Vanderbilt to supply service for the Niagara Falls power project. Both sides lobbied heavily for the contract and the choice of AC spelled the death of DC.

Direct current, however, has survived. Every time we use a battery-operated device we are using DC power, much to the pleasure of that bunny, who "just keeps on going and going..."

How did the disease cancer come to be named after a constellation of the zodiac?

Well, all you Cancerians out there can blame Hippocrates (remember him, of Hippocratic-oath fame?). It seems that back in the fifth century B.C. Hippocrates was treating a woman with a sore breast. He noticed large lumps from which radiated long, swollen veins that resembled little crabs. He called the disease "karkinos," Greek for crab. The disease later became known by its Latin name—cancer.

Where did we get the names of the days of the week?

Early England was a much-conquered country. The Romans and Saxons were two of the conquerors who left their mark on the development of the English language. Originally, all the days of the week had Roman names representing the planets. The Romans believed that the first hour of each day was ruled by a different planet, and the days of the week were named accordingly. After the Saxon invasions certain days were renamed for Teutonic gods. The name origins of the days of the week are listed below:

Sunday is an English translation of the Latin "Sun's Day," the old Teutonic people's sacred day of the sun.

Monday is from the Anglo-Saxon "Monan-daeg," meaning Moon's Day.

Tuesday is named in honor of the Teutonic god Tiw, the son of Woden.

Wednesday is named after the supreme Teutonic god Woden.

Thursday is named for Woden's son, Thor, god of thunder and lightning.

Friday is from the Anglo-Saxon "Frigg-daeg," named to honor Frigg, the wife of Woden and the goddess of marriage and love.

Saturday is from the Anglo-Saxon "Saeter-daeg," and named for the Roman god of Saturn, considered a day of bad omen.

The Quakers and more modern Israelis have a more exact, less pagan-influenced system for naming the days. They simply call them first day, second day, third day, etc. The Quakers are very practical, if not very romantic.

Why does orange juice taste funny after you brush your teeth?

It happens to all of us. You roll out of bed in the morning, brush your teeth and head downstairs for a nice sweet glass of orange juice. However, if you don't wait a short while, your OJ will taste rather funky.

This is due to a simple matter of chemistry. Most toothpastes contain the detergent sodium lauryl sulfate (SLS). Leftover SLS in your mouth makes sugar taste much less sweet than normal, and causes the acid in the juice to taste bitter. In a short while the excess SLS dissipates and your juice will taste just fine.

Most shampoos contain SLS and some also contain essence of orange. That would be an unusually bitter-tasting shampoo!

Why do you catch more colds in winter?

The most obvious answer, because it is cold outside, is erroneous. Scientific studies where one control group of people was kept damp and exposed to cold air and the other group was kept warm and dry showed no difference in the probability of catching cold. It is more likely that people get colds in winter for other reasons.

In the winter, people tend to stay indoors more, in proximity to each other and to each other's germs. Schools are in session and are breeding grounds for cold viruses. The air during the cold months is naturally a lot drier and when you put the heat on, you have superdry air. Superdry air means superdry sinuses. The nasal passages have a protective mucous membrane that doesn't function as well when it dries out.

Colds are caused by rhinoviruses. Most cold viruses enter your body through the nose. The rhinovirus (from the Greek "rhino," meaning nose) lands on the mucus membrane in the nasal passages and is swept to the back of the throat. Usually, cold viruses are destroyed upon entering the body. Either they are swallowed and killed by the stomach's digestive acids or are disposed of by the adenoids. Occasionally, however, a virus will lodge in the mucus membrane. The virus then enters a cell. Its DNA takes over the cell and forces the cell to crank out new copies of the virus, instead of new copies of the cell, as is supposed to happen. Within a few days of viral invasion you will have a full-blown cold, with the associated stuffy nose, sore throat, sneezing, and headache.

The average person will get at least one and possibly as many as six colds a year.

Since the biology of the cold virus is fairly well known, why can't scientists create a vaccine for it? After all, they can put a man on the moon! If colds were caused by one or two different rhinoviruses, there might well be a vaccine. However, there are over two hundred rhinoviruses, only about one hundred of which have been identified. Besides, colds are relatively minor ailments for the average person and the drug companies make a fortune selling antihistimines of dubious benefit.

Actually, it has been suggested that the side effects of antihistamines are worse than the cold symptoms they are supposed to lessen. Many people are injured or killed from the drowsiness and other adverse side effects of over-the-counter cold remedies. Just read the label of your favorite remedy sometime. There are more warnings on the label than you can shake a stick at.

Theoretically, you would never get a cold if you weren't exposed to the viruses. So how can you avoid contact with rhinoviruses? There are two schools of thought as to how the little buggers spread.

One theory says they travel through the air, borne on moisture droplets propelled by coughs and sneezes. When you sneeze, mucus (and virus)–laden air is shot out of your nose and mouth. So please cover up the next time you sneeze.

The other theory is that viruses are spread through touching things that a person with a cold has touched, like doorknobs, phones, etc. The virus can remain viable for several hours on these surfaces. When you touch a contaminated doorknob and then touch your nose or eyes, you are unknowingly inoculating yourself with the virus. If you are a believer in this theory, you can reduce your chances of getting a cold by washing your hands frequently during cold season and refraining from touching your nose or eyes. But don't become fanatical about this—you can't live your life in a bubble.

Why are the French referred to as "Frogs"?

The French have been called "Frogs" by outsiders for many centuries. The term "Frog" is rather derogatory and the French don't really appreciate its use. The word, however, originated in France.

France takes its name from the Franks, who ruled that region of Europe in the sixth century. The coat of arms of these Frankish rulers contained three golden toads. Therefore, the aristocracy of the time were called Toads. In contrast, the common citizens were known as Frogs, which was more or less a put down. The toads have since passed into history, but the nickname for the French, "Frogs," still remains.

How did the Los Angeles Dodgers come to be known by that unique name?

As all sports fans know, the Los Angeles Dodgers were once the Brooklyn Dodgers before they left New York City for tinseltown. What you may not know, is that they acquired the nickname "Dodgers" by virtue of the fact that the residents of Brooklyn were sarcastically referred to as "trolley dodgers" by the residents of Manhattan. At the turn of the century, Brooklyn was famous for its extensive trolley system, and the arrogant Manhattanites tagged Brooklynites with this unfavorable nickname. Various attempts were made to change the name from the Dodgers to the Robins, Superbas, and the Kings, but alas, the team was stuck with Dodgers.

Why the team retained the name Dodgers after they moved to Los Angeles is curious and rather silly, as is the Los Angeles Lakers retaining their nickname when they moved from Minneapolis. After all, Minnesota is the land of ten thousand lakes; Southern California is more like the land of ten thousand swimming pools!

Why are all scientific names for plants and animals in Latin?

Over 5 million different kinds of living organisms can be found on Earth. Many of them have common names, many don't. Common names, however, can be a little confusing. Two different regions can have the same name for completely different organisms.

For example, what we call a yam in the southern United States is totally different from the yams of the Caribbean area, and a pine in the United States is not the same thing as a pine in Australia. Therefore, to avoid confusion, a standard system of designation (nomenclature) was devised. Latin, because it is an ancient language and the basis for most Western languages, was the natural choice.

The practice began in medieval times, when Latin was the language of the scholarly. In this system, all roses would be designated *Rosa*, (the genus) with a short Latin description following to denote what kind of rose it was. This was kind of a long and awkward way to refer to plants. Then, in the eighteenth century, along came Carl von Linne. His ambition in life was to classify all the known plants and animals in the world. In 1753, he published his two-volume work, *Species Plantarum*, which listed every known plant by genus and introduced the one-word species name after, which came to replace the cumbersome Latin descriptions. This is what we call the binomial system of nomenclature that is universally used today. Linne was such a Latin enthusiast that he actually officially changed his "common" name, Carl von Linne, to the latinized Carolus Linnaeus. Trying to classify all the living organisms in the world would be enough to make anyone a little nutty.

Why did M&M/Mars discontinue the red M&M's candies for such a long time?

M&M's candies were an immediate hit upon their introduction in 1940. Named from the initials of their creators, Forest Mars, Sr., and Bruce Murrie, M&M's first big customer was the U.S. Army, who preferred the sugar-coated candies for the troops because they melted in the mouth but not in the hands. The multicolored candies have been popular favorites ever since.

M&M/MARS, however, discontinued the red candies in

its assortment of M&M's Chocolate Candies in the United States in 1976. They were not reintroduced into the M&M's color blend in the U.S. until 1987. There was much media attention and public misinformation surrounding the red dye used in red M&M's.

In 1976 the United States Food and Drug Administration delisted one particular red food coloring, FD&C No. 2 (amaranth), also known as Red Dye No. 2. The public was misled into believing that Red Dye No. 2 was a serious health concern and that red M&M's were colored with this dye. Horrified parents stopped buying M&M's and the company was forced by public opinion to cease the production of red M&M's.

However, M&M's Chocolate Candies never used Red Dye No. 2. The company simply removed the red candies to avoid consumer confusion and misplaced concerns. M&M/MARS did not take the red candies out of its Skittles Bite Size Candies because this product was not part of the misplaced media frenzy.

Interestingly enough, no other country that had Red Dye No. 2 on its approved list followed the FDA action, not even countries with very strict food and drug laws, such as Sweden and Canada. The FDA based its ban on studies by Soviet scientists, which were later found to be faulty. The red M&M's were never discontinued in any foreign country, and reappeared in the U.S. market in 1987 after persistent consumer complaints that they wanted their favorite M&M color back.

The red M&M's is not everyone's favorite, however. Surveys have found that brown is the general public's favorite M&M's color. The company created a color blend of candies that reflected consumer preference and gave a pleasing overall effect. Thus, the average blend contains 30 percent brown, 20 percent yellow, 20 percent red, 10 percent orange, 10 percent green, and 10 percent tan. For M&M's Peanut Chocolate Candies, the ratio is 20 percent each of brown, yellow, red, green, and orange. Consumer preference tests showed that the public doesn't care for tan peanut M&M's for some reason. While the company uses different dyes for each M&M's color, they all taste the same. Only the public's perceptions vary.

M&M/MARS uses all man-made colors because they resist fading, have a strong consistent hue, and impart no after-taste. Natural colorings do not possess these desirable qualities. If you think you can taste the difference between green and brown M&M's, you really can't. Try a blind taste test and see for yourself.

What are the origins of today's wedding rituals and customs?

An entire volume could be written on this subject, but in keeping with the limited scope of this book, we will look at just a few.

Nearly all of our modern wedding traditions have old and often silly roots, based on both superstition and fear.

Until recent times most marriages were prearranged by the parents, either to form desirable family mergers, or for financial gain. Love had very little to do with it. Marriage was also intended to produce offspring, and this was of paramount importance in most societies. Some cultures, like ancient Sparta, went so far as to fine single males. All cultures created some symbolic customs or rituals to ensure a couple's fruitfulness right from the start.

Timing of a wedding was considered critical in ancient Rome. The Romans preferred June weddings because this was the month they honored Juno, goddess of woman. They prayed to her to protect marriages and to ease childbirth. Roman weddings, like today's, were performed by a govern-ment magistrate (usually a woman), in front of witnesses. The bride's head was covered by a red veil to protect her from evil spirits. Iron rings and wheat cakes were exchanged. The couple was then showered with grain, symbolizing fertility, followed by a feast for all.

Other cultures added their beliefs to modern wedding customs. The Chinese believed that if the bride's shoes touched the ground bad luck would follow, so they rolled out a red carpet for her to walk on. This custom has evolved into today's bride walking on a white runner laid out from the limousine to the altar. The Scandinavians were also concerned with the bride's shoes and put a penny in her shoe for good fortune. Today's economy has brought the price of good luck up to a dime.

No wedding would be complete without wine, which has been present at feasts since time forgotten. The medieval French enjoyed their wine, although it wasn't as palatable as the vintages are today. To make the wine go down a little easier, they placed spiced pieces of toasted bread in the goblets. The first guest to drink his wine and swallow his bread earned the right to make a short speech, which, not surprisingly, became known as a toast to the bride.

Another popular wedding drink in Northern Europe was honey mead, or wine made from honey. The new couple were to drink a glass of this wine every day for the full cycle of the moon following the wedding day. During this time, "honey-moon," they were to stay hidden away from their parents.

One reason the couple had to hide away from the parents was that in some cases the bride was literally kidnapped by the groom and forced into a marriage. Women were scarce in some ancient villages and kidnapping was a good way to secure a wife. The best man helped with the "wife-napping" and stood at the side of the groom during the service, sword in hand, to ensure no one tried to prevent the ceremony. The groom would then take his bride into hiding, carrying her over the threshold of their new home, because she might not have wanted to enter willingly.

Why are golf courses called links, and why are golf bunkers filled with sand?

The game of golf originated in Scotland. The early courses were primitive by today's standards. Only the tees, fairways, and greens were grass. The rest of the course was either sand or scrub heath. The grass areas were said to have appeared to be links of green against the drab scrub and sand surroundings.

Golf courses near the seacoast were often the grazing grounds of wandering sheep. The sheep would frequently gather in depressions on the course for protection from the strong coastal winds. Their constant grazing of these depressions resulted in the same type of sandy traps and bunkers that have become common on most golf courses today.

Why are European wines considered better than American wines?

This is a tricky question, as there are now no totally pure European grape vines growing in Europe! In the nineteenth century there was a lot of exchanging back and forth of American and European grape varieties between the two continents for experimental growth. The Europeans unwittingly imported some American vines, which had uninvited guests that tagged along on the roots, the plant louse phylloxera. Native American vines are fairly immune to the louses' most devastating effects because the two evolved together and the vines developed a natural resistance—thick, hearty roots.

The European vine, *Vitis vinifera*, and its more delicate roots had never been exposed to phylloxera before and was decimated by this root pest. Almost all the world's best wine-grape vines were being wiped out. Europe had to act fast to save what was left of its wine industry, so they grafted the wine-producing vines of *Vitis vinifera* to the pest-resistant American root stocks.

Today, almost all European wines come from these European vines grafted on American roots, and so do many American wines. The only truly American wines come from New York State–grown varieties such as Delaware and Elvira, which are totally native American plants, roots, and vines.

Why does a Mexican jumping bean jump?

Mexican jumping beans are ordinary enough in and of themselves. The jumping phenomenon is caused by a moth larva (caterpillar) that is living inside the bean. One particular moth is partial to laying its eggs inside the flowers and beans of the Mexican bean plant. The movement of the caterpillar inside the bean makes it appear to jump. Heating the bean will agitate the larva, causing it to wiggle about, and the bean to jump.

At maturity the little fellow will spin a silk cocoon and turn into a moth. The moth will eventually emerge from the bean and start the life cycle all over again.

Why is it that bad breath from onions and garlic can stay with you for several hours, even after brushing teeth or gargling?

The word halitosis appeared in the British medical journal *Lancet* as a more scientific term than "bad breath." The Lambert Pharmacal Company, makers of Listerine, seized upon this word as a trendy term to use in promoting the bad breath–fighting qualities of their mouthwash. Mouthwash, however, does not remove the cause of bad breath but simply masks the odor. Bad breath can have several causes, such as trapped food debris in the mouth, rotting teeth, and lung or sinus infections.

Usually, however, bad breath is caused by the aromatic foods that we eat, such as onions or garlic. Oils from these foods, when digested, can enter the bloodstream and be transported to the lungs, where the odor is exhaled with our breathing. This is how you can have onion rings for lunch, brush your teeth before bed, and still be spurned by your spouse for having offensive breath.

Who coined the Maxwell House slogan "Good to the last drop"?

In 1873, a grocery salesman named Joel Cheek became interested in coffee and came up with his own unique blend. Realizing that he had created a fine brew, he decided to sell it. One of the South's best hotels, the Maxwell House, liked his coffee and began to serve it to guests; hence the name Maxwell House Coffee.

In 1907, on returning from a bear hunt in Mississippi, President Theodore Roosevelt was a guest of the Ladies Hermitage Association at Andrew Jackson's homestead in Nashville, Tennessee. He was served a cup of Maxwell

House Coffee. Upon being offered a refill, he remarked on the excellent quality of the coffee and uttered the now famous line, "Delightful. This coffee is good to the last drop."

Apparently when Roosevelt talked, people listened.

Was Dr. Seuss really a doctor?

Theodore Seuss Geisel, aka Dr. Seuss, was born in Springfield, Massachusetts, in 1904. He attended Dartmouth College and did graduate studies at Oxford University. However, he dropped out of college before receiving his Ph.D.

The pseudonym Dr. Seuss was perhaps wishful thinking on his part, using his middle name and the title of Doctor, which he had not earned at Oxford.

After graduate school, he tried to earn a living as a cartoonist in New York and was modestly successful. Then, in 1936, while sailing from England, he came up with a children's story that rhymed to the tempo of the ship's engines.

Interestingly, twenty-seven publishers rejected his first book, *And to Think I Saw It on Mulberry Street,* because it was a little too bizarre. Eventually a publisher took a chance, and the rest is history.

Most of us have grown up with Dr. Seuss books, and those of us with children probably now read these same books to our families. However, if you think books like *The Cat in the Hat* are simplistic and easy to write, think again. It took Geisel a year and a half to write and illustrate this book. His hard work paid off, as the *Cat* sold 500,000 copies in 1957, its first year in publication. All in all, Dr. Seuss published forty-eight books and sold more than 250 million copies.

Not bad for an author who, when at a loss for a good rhyme, would simply make up a silly new word to fit.

When is the North Pole not the North Pole?

When it is the South Pole, of course! As crazy as this may sound, the Earth's north magnetic pole and south magnetic pole occasionally reverse themselves. Over the last 4 million years or so, the Earth's magnetic fields have flipped at least nine times! The changes occur at random intervals and could happen at any time.

The Earth can be viewed as one giant magnet, with a north and south magnetic pole. If you put a piece of paper over a bar magnet and shake some iron filings over it, they will arrange themselves in the shape of the bar's magnetic field. The ones nearer the north pole point north, and the ones nearest the south pole point south.

The Earth has the same effect on the needle of a compass. In the Northern Hemisphere it points north and in the Southern Hemisphere it points south. In much the same way, minerals in molten rocks can become magnetized by Earth's magnetic field when they cool. As they harden they will align themselves toward the north magnetic pole. By studying the magnetic fields in ancient volcanic rock formations, such as basalt, scientists have learned that at certain times in history, all the basalt of a particular age had been magnetized to the south instead of the north. Since the rocks hadn't moved since their formation, the only explanation for the southward orientation is that the Earth's magnetic poles must have flip-flopped, causing the minerals to orient in the exact opposite direction.

No one knows how or why the Earth's magnetic poles flip. Its magnetic field is thought to be generated by its molten metal core. It could be that internal changes in the movements of the Earth's core cause the sudden change.

Does Heinz really have 57 varieties?

No! At one point the H. J. Heinz Company produced over twenty times that number of food products. Henry John

Heinz revolutionized the eating habits of late-nineteenth-century America.

It all started when Heinz, as a young boy, began growing horseradish in his family's garden. He sold the excess to neighbors. He then started selling it grated in vinegar. Horseradish was very popular because it made dull food palatable and added zip. After a couple of business failures he became very successful with the introduction of tomato ketchup in 1876. This was followed by green pepper sauce, white and cider vinegars, apple butter, chili sauce, mincemeat, mustard, tomato soup, olives, baked beans in tomato sauce, all sorts of pickles, and pickled vegetables. Heinz personally hit upon the "57 varieties" slogan.

One day in 1896, while riding the elevated train in New York City, he happened to see an advertisement boasting of 21 varieties of shoes and liked it. He actually had over 60 varieties at that time but just thought "57 varieties" had a certain ring to it.

Heinz's spicy products were warmly welcomed by an American public bored with eating the same basic, monotonous staples day after day.

In 1869, the average American diet was dull and bland for the better part of the year. Food staples included bread, root vegetables, potatoes, and smoked, dried, or salted meat. The only salads available in winter consisted of cucumbers, pickles, and leaf vegetables. Foodstuffs tended to remain in the region in which they were produced; only meats were shipped around the country.

Anyway, today Heinz has over 50 varieties of pickles alone. In fact, Heinz owns Star-Kist, Weight Watchers, Ore-Ida and 9-Lives and sells over three thousand products—a far cry from the original 57 varieties!

Why does the plant goldenrod cause hay fever?

Trick question! Goldenrod (*Solidago sp.*) does not cause hay fever. For years this much-maligned plant was blamed for causing hay fever symptoms, until it was realized that its pollen is not airborne, but is carried by bees and other insects.

Goldenrod is a genus of several species of flowering plants whose beautiful yellow flowers bloom from late summer to early fall.

People mistakenly assumed that the showy goldenrod was making them miserable, because it blooms at the same time that the real culprit, the relatively inconspicuous ragweed, blooms. The reason ragweed pollen causes hay fever, or allergic rhinitis, as it is properly called, has to do with its spiny shape. The pollen, referred to as an allergen, lodges in the sensitive sinus tissues when you unwittingly breathe it in. The body produces histamines that cause inflammation and fluid in the sinus, nose, and eyes. Antihistamines can alleviate the symptoms, or you can try to avoid the allergen, although that may prove to be impossible.

If you have hay fever, you may actually be allergic to grass pollen if your symptoms occur in the early summer, tree pollen if they occur in spring, or ragweed if they occur in late summer.

Hay fever is probably inherited and may spontaneously occur later in life with no previous warning.

Why can you often hear distant AM radio stations at night, but not during the day?

If you have ever flipped round the AM dial after dark, you may have been amazed to hear a radio station several hundred or even thousands of miles away. However, try to get the same station the next day, and you can't find it. This phenomenon is due to the weird ability of the ionosphere to reflect AM radio waves back to Earth. The ionosphere is an electrified region of the upper atmosphere where large concentrations of ions and free electrons exist. The lower ionosphere reflects AM radio waves back to Earth. Other radio waves with shorter wavelengths can penetrate this layer and are reflected back by the upper ionosphere. FM radio waves, radar, television, and visible light are too short to be reflected by the ionosphere at all.

Radio waves travel in a straight line. Due to the curvature of the Earth, radio waves usually can only reach receivers within a hundred-mile radius of the transmitter before they are sent into space. AM radio waves, however, can bounce off the ionosphere and travel greater distances around the surface of the Earth, but only at night. During daylight hours, free electrons in the lower atmosphere absorb and weaken AM radio waves as they are reflected. This weakening effect is strongest during the day because energy from the sun is the main cause for the presence of free electrons. After dark, these electrons readily combine with positive ions, greatly reducing the absorption of the radio waves. Since absorption is lessened at night, the AM radio waves can bounce back and forth between the ionosphere and the Earth without a significant loss of energy. Thus, they can travel hundreds of additional miles at night. For this reason, AM radio stations must reduce their power output to avoid interfering with distant radio stations that broadcast at the same frequency.

Ham radio operators use shortwaves to communicate over thousands of miles during both day and night. Because they use shorter waves, their wavelengths can penetrate the lower ionosphere and be reflected back to Earth by the upper ionosphere.

Why have Native Americans (until recently) always been called Indians when they do not come from India, and why are Americans named after a man who did not discover them?

As you probably know, when Christopher Columbus set out on his historic journey, in 1492, he had no intention of discovering a New World, but simply wanted to find a new route to the East Indies (that area of Asia which includes

India, Indochina, Malaya, and the Malay archipelago). Columbus was so consumed with reaching the Orient by sailing west from Europe, that he refused to believe the islands he had landed on in the Caribbean were not part of the East Indies. Despite repeated visits to the area, he found no actual proof that he was in the Orient, but his enormous ego would not allow him to admit that he had failed in his quest. The Spanish government, Columbus's sponsor, wasn't as sure as Columbus that he had indeed reached the Orient. However, for lack of a better name, the government officially referred to their new empire as the "Indies." They therefore christened its inhabitants as "Indians."

Like so many other things named throughout history, the first name often sticks, regardless of accuracy. Today we know better, and should refer to American Indians as Native Americans, and to people from India as Indians.

America got its name at roughly the same time in history. It is named after the Italian explorer Amerigo Vespucci. He traveled to the New World, first under the Spanish flag, and later under the rival Portuguese flag. Vespucci was personally acquainted with Columbus and helped in the preparation of some of his ships. Between 1497 and 1504, Vespucci set out to realize Columbus's failed dream of sailing west to the Indies. On his several voyages, first as a navigator and then as a captain, Vespucci sailed up and down the coast of South America. It was on his journey of 1501–1502 that he came to realize that these "Indies" of Columbus, were in fact, a new continent. He was not the egomaniac that Columbus was. Thus, his mind was flexible enough to enable him to make his great realization. Stubborn Columbus went to his deathbed convinced that he had reached the Orient.

Contrary to popular belief, Vespucci did not name America after himself. Vespucci's discoveries were published in a French letter entitled "Four Voyages." An obscure clergyman, Martin Waldseemüller, who had an interest in geography, was greatly influenced by this account of Vespucci's travels. He published a book of cosmography, a kind of atlas, in 1507. In it, he introduced a fourth continent as described by Amerigo Vespucci. He credited Vespucci with the discovery of the New World and called this area America in honor of its discoverer. The first two editions of the book were rapid sellers. Prior to publication of the third edition, Waldseemüller changed his mind about crediting Vespucci for the discovery of the New World and had the name America deleted from subsequent editions. However, it was too late to change peoples' minds. Another new word had been introduced to the language.

And, while Columbus's birthday is a national holiday and uncounted statues in the Western Hemisphere honor him, there is probably not one statue or plaque recognizing Amerigo Vespucci, the man for whom the New World was named.

Is there really a person named Jethro Tull?

Most younger people have heard of the musical group Jethro Tull and most rock 'n' roll fans know that there is no one in the band named Jethro Tull. The leader of the band is an Englishman, Ian Anderson. The band is named after an English gentleman farmer, Jethro Tull. Tull helped revolutionize farming practices in the early eighteenth century. His invention of a drill for boring straight holes for planting seeds into was a great improvement over the wasteful practice of throwing the seeds and letting them land randomly. He also showed that frequent hoeing of the soil helps to keep it fertile. One wonders how he would have felt about his name being used to front such songs as "Aqualung" and "Locomotive Breath."

Why is the ocean salty?

The ocean is the eventual depository for most of Earth's water. Over the eons of land and ocean formation, dissolved minerals from Earth's crust were washed into the ocean. As time went on, water was continuously evaporating from the ocean, leaving behind mineral salts until they reached their present-day concentrations.

Salt water is roughly 3.5 percent dissolved mineral salts, much of which is sodium chloride, ordinary table salt. Fresh water contains dissolved mineral salts too, but at concentrations too low for us to taste.

Salt lakes often are found in a region where the rate of evaporation is high and dissolved salts are left behind. These are closed lake systems, because there is no drainage. One famous lake, which is saltier than the ocean, is the Great Salt Lake in the state of Utah. The Dead Sea has a 25 percent salt content, so high that, due to buoyancy it is almost impossible to drown.

Why do men go bald, but not most women?

Some men would pay any amount of money not to be bald. A cure has been sought for centuries. Baldness may occur from several causes (e.g. disease, radiation exposure, thyroid imbalance); however, normal pattern baldness is genetically controlled, through sex-influenced genes.

Pattern baldness is much more prevalent in men but does occur in women. However, women generally experience a thinning of their hair, not complete hair loss on top of the head. Some daily hair loss is perfectly natural. Each of us loses between 25 and 125 hairs a day. As long as they are being replaced there is no need for concern.

We all have two genes for baldness. Each gene is either a dominant (B) or a recessive gene (b). We get one gene from each parent and we can inherit them in three possible combinations—BB, Bb or bb. Gene B is dominant for baldness in males and recessive in females. Males have a hormone that triggers baldness in the presence of only one B-gene. This means that a man needs only one B-gene to be bald (i.e. BB or Bb). Females, however, require both B-genes

(BB) to exhibit baldness. Males or females with two recessive genes (bb) will not be bald.

Are you confused yet?

The following illustrates the possibilities:

Genes	Male	Female
BB	Bald	Bald
Bb	Bald	Not bald
bb	Not bald	Not bald

From this chart you can see that a nonbald mother (Bb) can give her son a B-gene, thus causing him to be bald regardless of the father's hair condition.

A parallel example of sex-influenced genes in the animal world is the presence of horns in sheep (dominant in males); and hair color in cattle (mahogany and white dominant in males, red and white dominant in females).

If you are a young man worried about your potential for hair loss, take note. There seems to be a correlation between the amount of chest hair you have and your chances for future baldness. The hormones that produce chest hair also control male pattern baldness. So at age thirty, the more hair you have on your chest, the less you will have on your head at age forty.

Why does the U.S. Postal Service issue so many different stamp designs?

The U.S. Postal Service is constantly creating and issuing new stamp designs. One would think if you have a nicely designed twenty-nine cent stamp, that it should be sufficient to last until the next increase in stamp prices, which happens frequently. After all, the U.S. Treasury Department doesn't issue newly designed dollar bills every year or so. Well, the Postal Service has a very cost-effective and lucrative reason for doing so.

There is a great demand from business customers, stamp collectors, and the general public for the issuing of a variety of designs. Business customers, who use the Postal Service more than any other sector of society, experience a 2 to 3 percent response to mailings when they use stamps. However, the response rate falls to 1/2 percent when these same businesses use bulk mail (no stamps). Apparently, junk mail is more inviting when one sees a nice stamp on the envelope. So, when these businesses suggest that stamp subjects should vary, the Postal Service listens.

The Postal Service printed 40 billion stamps in 1991, 5 percent of which were commemorative stamps. These are prized by stamp collectors.

"Commemorative" issues usually honor historical figures or events and are more elaborate in their design and printing than are the "definitive" issues. Definitive issues are usually printed in two colors and in quantities of hundreds of millions over several years. They support third-class mailings and always include at least one definitive flag issue. Commemoratives, however, are issued in quantities of about 150 million and are available for up to a year.

Although producing numerous designs for collectors is more expensive than producing one design, these issues realize an enormous profit for the Postal Service. It costs one third of one cent to make a twenty-nine cent stamp. So, to issue the 2 billion annually produced commemorative stamps costs just $5 million, while yielding $180 million in revenues. However, collectors hoard these stamps. They are seldom touched by human tongues.

As a result, no delivery service is rendered—although it is theoretically paid for. In order to please collectors, stamps are designed by artists to be as close to a work of art as possible. The 1992 Elvis Presley stamp "election" demonstrated the public's philatelic interest. While the "young Elvis" won out over the old, one wonders why they just didn't issue both images. (Perhaps it was just to increase public interest and, therefore, sales.)

Why is Rhode Island so named, when it is not an island?

No one is certain, but one theory credits French explorer Giovanni da Verrazano. He was searching up and down the East Coast in vain for a northwest passage to the Pacific Ocean in 1524. Supposedly, Verrazano noted an island (probably Aquidneck Island) and recorded in his journal that it was about the size of the island of Rhodes in the Mediterranean. Subsequently, it became known as Rhode Island.

Another theory is that Rhode Island got its name from Dutch explorer Adriaen Block. He sighted an island in what is now Narragansett Bay. Block called the island "Roodt Eylandt," Dutch for "red island," because of its red clay.

Rhode Islanders are still big on the color red. The state tree is the red maple and the state bird is the Rhode Island Red.

Settlers who sought religious and political freedom from Massachusetts migrated to Rhode Island. The first two colonies were established at Providence, in 1636, and on Aquidneck Island in 1638. In 1644, these and other nearby colonies joined to form one colony, known as Providence Plantations. Later that year, Aquidneck Island became known as the Isle of Rhodes, or Rhode Island. In 1663, the entire colony was renamed "Rhode Island and Providence Plantations." Its official name today is "The State of Rhode Island and Providence Plantations." Hence, the seemingly inappropriate nickname, the Plantation State.

Are hard leather shoes really better for babies' feet?

Not really. Here's another case where you were right and Mom was wrong. Those stiff, uncomfortable saddle shoes you had to endure wearing as a child, supposedly for proper support, were probably more harmful than beneficial.

Just as nature intended, bare feet are the best for normal foot development. Shoes, for most children, are intended to do nothing more than keep the feet warm, dry, and protected from sharp objects. These "support" shoes, which some of us were forced to wear, can retard a child's natural walking and foot development and may actually delay walking or encourage foot problems, like toe-in or toe-out. Sneakers, as logic dictates, are more comfortable and allow most babies' feet to grow unhindered by artificial restrictions. So do your baby a favor and buy him or her sneakers, or better yet, let baby go barefoot whenever possible. (Many children do, however, have foot problems and can benefit from orthopedic shoes. Consult your child's pediatrician if you are in doubt.)

Why do those little white doughnut-shaped blips appear occasionally in the upper-right-hand corner of movies and old TV shows?

The next time you go to the movies, see if you notice a ring-shaped object flash in the upper right-hand corner, and then, a short time later, another one will follow, during the film. These blips aren't flaws in the film or subliminal messages to go out and buy doughnuts. They are cues to the projectionist to change film reels. The first one is a warning to get ready, the second one is to roll the next reel.

These reel-change indicators are rough circles scratched into the upper right-hand corner of ten or fifteen consecutive frames. Movies are projected at twenty-four frames per second, so these marks appear for about half a second. You can tell a new reel has begun because immediately after the second cue, the movie jumps to another scene or camera angle. Most of us are so intent on the movie action that we rarely take notice.

What is the origin of April Fools' Day?

Different versions of an All Fools' Day have been observed around the globe for several centuries. One example is the Indian feast of Huli, held each year near the spring equinox on March 31. It is celebrated by sending people on foolish errands. It is thought to have its roots in the Roman Cerealia festival held in early April to ensure a good planting. According to Roman mythology, the goddess Proserpina had filled her lap with daffodils. Pluto found her and carried her, screaming, back to the underworld. Her mother, Ceres, went looking for her, following the echoes of her screams. This was a fool's errand because it is impossible to find an echo.

All Fools' Day is thought to have started in France in the fifteenth century. Someone fooled on April 1, in France, is called a *poisson d'avril,* or April Fish, because fish are easily caught in early April. It wasn't until the early 1700s that the custom moved to England. The tradition was carried to the United States with the early settlers.

Is it true that Babe Ruth once "called" a home run?

The home run that Babe Ruth blasted at Chicago's Wrigley Field, in the fifth inning of the third game of the 1932 World

Series, is one of the most fabled stories in sports history. It was Ruth's last World Series homer, and is the one that helped turn him into a baseball legend. Whether the story is entirely true, however, is doubtful.

The Cubs had lost the first two games of the series at Yankee Stadium, and the Chicago players and fans were taunting the Babe during the first game at Wrigley Field. Ruth came to the plate in the fifth inning, with the score tied 4–4, to face Cubs' pitcher Charlie Root. Ruth swung at, and missed, Root's first two pitches and the crowd loved it. Root's next two pitches were balls and the fans booed the Babe for not swinging at them. This much of the story appears to be factual. What happened next, however, is unclear. Some eyewitnesses say that Ruth pointed toward the Chicago dugout as a warning to calm down. Others claim he pointed defiantly at Root. Still others say Ruth held up one finger (not the middle one!) to indicate to the fans that it only takes one swing to knock the ball out of the park. All these explanations of what happened seem ordinary and believable. However, baseball legend has it that the Babe pointed to the spot in center field where he intended to hit the next pitch. Sure enough, he sent the next pitch over the center field wall, right where he had indicated.

A sportswriter at the game, Paul Gallico, may be responsible for starting this legend. Gallico reported that Ruth "pointed like a duelist to the spot where he expected to send his rapier home." Gallico wouldn't have been the first reporter to embellish upon the accomplishments of this larger-than-life American hero.

Whether or not Babe actually predicted this home run is really academic. He remains the greatest all-around baseball player who ever lived. His sixty home runs in a 154-game season have never been topped. (In 1961, Roger Maris had fifty-nine homers after his first 154 games, but reached sixty-one after 162 games.) He led the American League in homers twelve times. His home run percentage was higher than any other player (8.5 percent), and his lifetime total (714) was only topped by Hank Aaron (755), who needed an additional 3,965 times at bat to reach that number (6.1 percent). Ruth finished with a .342 lifetime batting average.

Ruth was also a marvelous pitcher early in his career. He once pitched 29^2/$_3$ scoreless innings for the Boston Red Sox in the 1916 and 1918 World Series. He was the best left-handed American League pitcher, until he was moved to the outfield so that he could play and bat in every game.

About the Author

Don Voorhees has collected interesting stories and bits of information continually over the years and claims to have never lost at a game of Trivial Pursuit. Contained here in his first book is the result of countless hours of reading and PBS viewing. He lives in Easton, Pennsylvania, with his wife, Lisa, and their two children, Eric and Dana.